PLAYS BY PETER WEISS

The Investigation 1966
The Persecution and Assassination of JEAN-PAUL MARAT *as
    Performed by the Inmates of the Asylum of Charenton
    under the Direction of the* MARQUIS DE SADE 1965

THE INVESTIGATION

THE INVESTIGATION

A PLAY BY

PETER WEISS

ENGLISH VERSION BY

JON SWAN AND ULU GROSBARD

ATHENEUM NEW YORK 1981

All inquiries concerning the rights for professional or
amateur stock production should be directed to
Joan Daves, 515 Madison Avenue, New York, N.Y. 10022

CHARACTERS

JUDGE

PROSECUTING ATTORNEY

COUNSEL FOR THE DEFENSE

1ST WITNESS

2ND WITNESS

3RD WITNESS

4TH WITNESS

5TH WITNESS

6TH WITNESS

7TH WITNESS

8TH WITNESS

9TH WITNESS

ACCUSED #1   ADJUTANT MULKA

ACCUSED #2   BOGER

ACCUSED #3   DR CAPESIUS

ACCUSED #4   DR FRANK

ACCUSED #5   DR SCHATZ

ACCUSED #6   DR LUCAS

ACCUSED #7   KADUK

ACCUSED #8   HOFMANN

ACCUSED #9   MEDICAL ORDERLY KLEHR

ACCUSED #10 SCHERPE

ACCUSED #11 HANTL

ACCUSED #12 S.S. CORPORAL STARK

ACCUSED #13 BARETZKI

ACCUSED #14 SCHLAGE

ACCUSED #15 BISCHOF

ACCUSED #16 BROAD

ACCUSED #17 BREITWIESER

ACCUSED #18 BEDNAREK

NOTE

In the presentation of this play, no attempt should be made to reconstruct the courtroom before which the proceedings of the camp trial took place. Any such reconstruction would, in the opinion of the author, be as impossible as trying to present the camp itself on the stage.

Hundreds of witnesses appeared before the court. The confrontations of witnesses and the accused, as well as the addresses to the court by the prosecution and the replies by the counsel for the defense, were overcharged with emotion.

Only a condensation of the evidence can remain on the stage.

This condensation should contain nothing but facts. Personal experience and confrontations must be steeped in anonymity. Inasmuch as the witnesses in the play lose their names, they become mere speaking tubes. The nine witnesses sum up what hundreds expressed.

The variety of experiences can, at most, be indicated by a change of voice or bearing.

Witnesses 1 and 2 are witnesses who worked with the camp administration.

Witnesses 4 and 5 are female, the rest male witnesses from the ranks of the surviving prisoners.

Each of the 18 accused, on the other hand, represents a single and distinct figure. They bear names taken from the record of the actual trial. The fact that they bear their own names is significant, since they also did so during the time of the events under consideration, while the prisoners had lost their names.

Yet the bearers of these names should not be accused once again in this drama.

To the author, they have lent their names which, within the drama, exist as symbols of a system that implicated in its guilt many others who never appeared in court.

THE INVESTIGATION

THE SONG OF THE PLATFORM

I

JUDGE: The witness
                  was stationmaster of the railroad station
                  where the trains arrived
                  How far was the station from the camp

1ST WITNESS: A mile and a quarter from the old army camp
                  About three miles from the main camp

JUDGE: Did your work take you into the camp

1ST WITNESS: No
                  I only had to make sure
                  that the tracks in use were in good condition
                  and that the trains arrived and departed
                  according to schedule

JUDGE: Were you in charge of
                  setting up the train schedules

1ST WITNESS: No
                  I only had to take care of technical measures
                  related to scheduling the shuttle traffic
                  between the station and the camp

JUDGE: The record contains scheduling orders
                  bearing your signature

1ST WITNESS: It's possible that in the absence

3

of the officer in charge
I occasionally had to sign one

JUDGE: Were you aware
of the purpose of the transport

1ST WITNESS: I wasn't informed on that matter

JUDGE: You knew
that the trains were loaded with people

1ST WITNESS: All we were told
was that it had to do
with relocation transports
carried out under government orders

JUDGE: Didn't it seem strange to you
that the trains returning
from the camp were always empty

1ST WITNESS: The people forwarded
had been relocated there

PROSECUTING
ATTORNEY: At present
you hold a high executive position
in the management
of the government railways
Therefore we may assume
that you are acquainted with the equipment
and loading capacity of trains
How were the trains
that arrived in your station
equipped and loaded

1ST WITNESS: The trains in question were freight trains

According to the bills of lading
some 60 persons were forwarded in each car

PROSECUTING
ATTORNEY: Were the cars freight cars
or were they cattle cars

1ST WITNESS: Some of the cars were the kind
used to ship cattle
PROSECUTING
ATTORNEY: Were there any sanitary installations
in the cars

1ST WITNESS: I don't know
PROSECUTING
ATTORNEY: How often did these trains arrive

1ST WITNESS: I couldn't say
PROSECUTING
ATTORNEY: Did they arrive frequently

1ST WITNESS: Yes
Sure
It was a very busy terminal
PROSECUTING
ATTORNEY: Didn't it strike you
that the trains
came from almost every country in Europe

1ST WITNESS: We had so much to do
There wasn't any time to worry about
things like that
PROSECUTING
ATTORNEY: Did you ever wonder about
what was going to happen
to the people in those trains

1ST WITNESS: We heard they were being shipped in
for supplementary labor

PROSECUTING
ATTORNEY: But there weren't only people fit for work
but whole families
with old people and children

1ST WITNESS: I didn't have time
to check the contents of the trains

PROSECUTING
ATTORNEY: Where did you live

1ST WITNESS: In the town
PROSECUTING
ATTORNEY: Who else lived there

1ST WITNESS: The town had been cleared
of its original population
Camp officials lived there
and personnel from surrounding industries

PROSECUTING
ATTORNEY: What kind of industries were those

1ST WITNESS: They were branch plants
of I-G Farben
Krupp and Siemens

PROSECUTING
ATTORNEY: Did you see the prisoners
who had to work there

1ST WITNESS: I saw them
when they marched to work and back

PROSECUTING
ATTORNEY: What condition were they in

1ST WITNESS: They marched in step and they sang

PROSECUTING
ATTORNEY: You didn't hear anything
                about conditions in the camp

1ST WITNESS: There were so many insane rumors going
                    around
                you never knew what to think
PROSECUTING
ATTORNEY: You heard nothing
                about the annihilation of people there

1ST WITNESS: How could anybody believe a thing like that

JUDGE: The witness was responsible
                for the delivery of the freight

2ND WITNESS: All I had to do was
                turn the trains over to the shunting crew

JUDGE: What were their duties

2ND WITNESS: They hitched the switch engine onto the trains
                and took them on into the camp

JUDGE: How many people would you estimate
                were there in each car

2ND WITNESS: I can't provide you with any information
                on that matter
                We were strictly forbidden
                to examine the trains

JUDGE: Who prevented you

2ND WITNESS: The guards

JUDGE:	Were there bills of lading for all the transports
2ND WITNESS:	In most cases there were no bills attached There was only the number chalked up on the freight car
JUDGE:	What were the numbers
2ND WITNESS:	60 or 80 head It varied
JUDGE:	When did the trains arrive
2ND WITNESS:	Mainly at night
PROSECUTING ATTORNEY:	What impression did you get of the freight
2ND WITNESS:	I don't understand the question
PROSECUTING ATTORNEY:	As superintendent of the government railroads you are undoubtedly familiar with travel conditions Didn't you get some idea of conditions by looking in through air vents or by hearing sounds coming from the cars
2ND WITNESS:	Once I saw a woman holding a small child up to the air vent and calling out over and over for some water I got a pitcher of water

I started to lift it up to her
when one of the guards came over
and said
if I didn't leave at once
I would be shot

JUDGE: How many trains would you estimate
arrived in the station daily

2ND WITNESS: On the average a train a day
When the pressure was on
two or three

JUDGE: How long were the trains

2ND WITNESS: They had up to 60 cars

JUDGE: Were you ever
in the camp

2ND WITNESS: I went in with the switch engine once
because there was something
to clear up in the bill of lading
Just back of the entrance gate I got off
and went into the camp office
I almost didn't get out of there either
because I didn't have my pass with me

JUDGE: Did you see anything of the camp

2ND WITNESS: Nothing
I was just glad to get out of there

JUDGE: Did you see the chimneys
at the end of the platform
or the smoke and glare

2ND WITNESS: Yes
I saw smoke

JUDGE: And what did you think

2ND WITNESS: I thought
those must be the bakeries
I had heard
they baked bread in there day and night
After all it was a big camp

THE SONG OF THE PLATFORM

II

3RD WITNESS: We traveled five days
On the second day
our provisions were used up
There were 89 of us in the freight car
Our suitcases and bundles besides
We relieved ourselves
in the straw
Many were sick
and eight were dead
At the stations along the way
we could look out through the air vents
and see the women personnel
handing food and coffee up to the guards
Our children had stopped crying
when on the last night we were switched
off the main track onto a siding
We passed through a flat region
lit up by searchlights
Then we came up along a very long
building like a shed
There was a tower
and under it an archway
The locomotive whistled
before we went in under the arch
The train stopped
The freight-car doors were pulled open
Prisoners in striped uniforms appeared
and yelled in at us
Out

Move
Fast
Fast
It was four feet down to the ground
The ground was broken rock
The old people and the sick fell
onto the sharp stones
The dead and the luggage
were thrown out of the cars
Then we heard
Leave everything where it is
Women and children there
Men on the other side
I lost sight of my family
All around
people were shouting for
their families their relatives
They were being beaten with clubs
Dogs were barking
Searchlights and machine guns were trained
at us from the observation towers
At the end of the platform was the sky
glowing red
The air was full of smoke
The smoke had a sweet singed smell
From then on
this smoke was always there

4TH WITNESS: I could still hear my husband
calling me
We were lined up
and were not permitted to change places
We were a group
of 100 women and children
We stood five in a row
Then we had to walk past some officers

One of them held his hand at chest level
and pointed his finger
left then right
The children and old women
went to the left
I went to the right
The left group had to cross the tracks
to get over to a road
I saw my mother for just a second
She was in the group with the children
That made me feel a bit easier
and I thought
we'll manage to get together again
A woman next to me said
They're going to a rehabilitation camp
She pointed to the trucks
parked on the road
and a Red Cross car
We could see
them being loaded into a truck
and we were glad they could ride again
The rest of us had to go
down the muddy road on foot

5TH WITNESS: I held my sister-in-law's child
by the hand
My sister-in-law
was holding her smallest child
in her own arms
Then one of the prisoners came up to me
and asked if the child was mine
when I said it wasn't
he said I should give it to its mother
I did and I thought
perhaps mothers got special consideration
They all went off to the left

I went to the right
The officer who divided us
was very friendly
I asked him
where the others were going
and he said
They're just going to shower now
You'll see them again in an hour

JUDGE: Does the witness
                 know who this officer was

5TH WITNESS: I found out later
                 that his name was Dr Capesius

JUDGE: Can the witness tell us
                 which of the accused is Dr Capesius

5TH WITNESS: When I look at their faces
                 I find it hard to tell
                 whether I recognize them or not
                 But that man there
                 looks familiar to me

JUDGE: What is his name

5TH WITNESS: Dr Capesius

ACCUSED #3:   The witness must have confused me
                 with someone else
                 I never took part in the selections
                 on the platform

6TH WITNESS: I had known Dr Capesius from my hometown
                 I was a doctor
                 and before the war

he used to call on me frequently
as a representative of the Bayer concern
On the platform I greeted him and asked
what was going to happen to us
He said
Everything's going to be fine here
I told him
my wife was not well
Then she should stand over there
he said
She will receive medical attention there
He pointed to the group
of old people and children
I told my wife
You go over there and get in line
She went over with her niece
and a couple of other relatives
to where the sick stood
They were all taken away in trucks

JUDGE: There is no doubt in your mind
               that that man was Dr Capesius

6TH WITNESS: No
               I spoke with him
               At the time it was a great pleasure for me
               to see him again

JUDGE: Accused Capesius
               do you know this witness

ACCUSED #3:   No

JUDGE: Were you present on the platform
               for the arrival of transports

ACCUSED #3:   I was only there
               to receive the medical supplies
               from the prisoners' luggage
               I had to store these supplies
               in the dispensary

JUDGE: Whom else among the accused
               did you see on the platform

6TH WITNESS: Him
               I remember his name
               His name is Hofmann

JUDGE: Accused Hofmann
               what were your duties on the platform

ACCUSED #8:   I was there to keep peace and order

JUDGE: How did you do that

ACCUSED #8:   The people were lined up
               Then the doctors decided
               who was fit for work
               and who wasn't
               Sometimes there were more
               and sometimes less
               The percentage was decided beforehand
               It was determined by the need
               for manpower at the time

JUDGE: What happened to those
               who were not used for work

ACCUSED #8:   They were gassed

JUDGE: What percent of the people
               was fit for work

16

ACCUSED #8: On the average
one third of a transport
When the camp was overloaded
transports went straight through
without being opened

JUDGE: Did you yourself
carry out any selections

ACCUSED #8: All I can say
is that sometimes
when they begged me to
I pushed some of the unfit
over to the fit group

JUDGE: Were you allowed to do that

ACCUSED #8: No
It was against regulations
but we closed our eyes to it

JUDGE: Were special rations issued
for men assigned to platform duty

ACCUSED #8: Yes
We got bread
a portion of sausage
and a half pint of brandy

JUDGE: In the performance of your duties
did you ever need to resort to force

ACCUSED #8: There was always a lot of confusion
and naturally sometimes
somebody had to be straightened out
or slapped

I only did my duty
Whatever I'm assigned to do
I do my duty

JUDGE: How did you get this assignment

ACCUSED #8:   By accident
It was like this
My brother had an extra uniform
I could use
So it didn't cost me anything
Then there were business reasons
My father had a restaurant
that a lot of party members used to come to
When I was sent off
I had no idea
where I would end up
When I got to the camp I asked
Am I really in the right place
They told me
You're in the right place here all right

PROSECUTING
ATTORNEY: Did you know what would happen
to the people who were selected

ACCUSED #8:   Mr Prosecutor
I personally didn't have anything
against those people
There were some like them at home too
Before they were taken away
I always used to tell my family
You go right on buying from them
After all they are human too

PROSECUTING
ATTORNEY: Was that still your attitude
when you were doing platform duty

ACCUSED #8: Well
except for small troubles
like you get whenever
you have a lot of people in a small place
and except for the gassings
which naturally were terrible
still
everybody had a chance to survive
Personally
I always behaved decently
Anyway what could I do
Orders are orders
And now just because I obeyed
I've got this trial hung on my neck
Mr Prosecutor
I've always tried to live in peace
just like everybody else
and then suddenly I'm hauled out
and everybody starts yelling about Hofmann
That's the one that's Hofmann
they say
What do they want from me

7TH WITNESS: When we were all lined up
one of the guards came and asked
Does anyone have any physical handicap
A few people stepped forward
They thought
they would get easier work that way
They were sent over to those
who had to go to the left
When the guard led them off
there was a disturbance
and he started shooting
Five or six people were killed

JUDGE: Does the witness see

the person he has been speaking of
in this room

7TH WITNESS: Your Honor
it has been many years
since I last stood in front of them
and I find it hard
to look them in the face
That one looks like him
That could be him
His name is Bischof

JUDGE: Are you sure
or do you have any doubts

7TH WITNESS: Your Honor
I could not sleep at all last night

COUNSEL FOR
THE DEFENSE: We question the credibility
of the witness
It may be assumed
that he recognized the face of our client
from pictures published in the press
Certainly the exhaustion of the witness
is in itself no proof
of the validity of his testimony

JUDGE: Would the accused Bischof
care to take a stand
in regard to the accusation

ACCUSED #15:I frankly can't understand
just what the witness is trying to say
I don't understand either
why he says

five or six
If he had said five
or if he had said six
one or the other
then I could understand it

JUDGE: Were you assigned to platform duty

ACCUSED #15: All I had to do
             was to organize the prisoners into groups
             I never did any shooting
             Your Honor
             all I would really like to do here
             is make a clean breast of everything
             It has been troubling me deeply for years
             I have developed heart trouble
             from all the worry
             And then they have to foul up
             the last years of my life
             with this whole stinking mess

PROSECUTING
ATTORNEY: What stinking mess is
             the accused referring to

JUDGE: The accused is excited
             Certainly he can scarcely be referring to
             the proceedings
             initiated by the attorney general
                  [*The Accused laugh*]

8TH WITNESS: As a prisoner
             I belonged to the clean-up detail
             Our job was
             to carry off the luggage of the arrivals
             The accused Baretzki
             took part in the selections on the platform

and he accompanied
the trains to the crematoriums

JUDGE: Do you recognize the accused

8TH WITNESS: That is Barrack-leader Baretzki

ACCUSED #13: I only belonged to the guard unit
             For a guard to do the selecting
             was out of the question
             A barrack-leader could not select the unfit
             on his own
             Only a doctor could do that

JUDGE: Were you aware of the purpose
             of the selections

ACCUSED #13: We heard about it
             I was deeply shocked
             Once when I was home on leave
             I told my mother about it
             She wouldn't believe it
             That's impossible
             she said
             Anyway people don't burn
             because you can't burn flesh

8TH WITNESS: I saw
             how Baretzki pointed out the people
             with his swagger stick
             Things never went fast enough for him
             He always tried to speed them up
             Once a train loaded with 3000 people
             came in
             Most of them were sick

Baretzki yelled at us
You've got 15 minutes
to get them out of there
A baby was born during the unloading
I wrapped it in a piece of cloth
and set it down by the mother
Baretzki came at me with his stick
and beat me and the woman
What are you doing with that garbage there
he yelled
and he kicked the baby
so it flew about 10 yards
Then he ordered
Bring that shit over here
By then the child was dead

JUDGE: Can you swear to that

8TH WITNESS: I can swear to that
                Baretzki had a special way of hitting
                He chopped
                He was known for it

JUDGE: What was it like

8TH WITNESS: He did it with the flat of his hand
                Like so
                Against the aorta
                In most cases
                it resulted in death

ACCUSED #13:   But the witness just got through saying
                that I had a stick
                Now if I had a stick
                surely
                there was no need for me

to hit with my hand
And if I used my hand
then I wouldn't need the stick
Your Honor
the whole thing is a slander
I didn't have any special chop at all
　　　[*The Accused laugh*]

THE SONG OF THE PLATFORM
III

JUDGE: Who else did you see on the platform

8TH WITNESS: All the doctors were out on the platform
The selections were part of their work
Dr Frank was there
Dr Schatz and Dr Lucas

COUNSEL FOR
THE DEFENSE: Where were you
while the selections were being made

8TH WITNESS: At various points on the platform
picking up suitcases

COUNSEL FOR
THE DEFENSE: Can you give us a description
of the platform

8TH WITNESS: The platform was behind the entrance gates
To the right of the platform
was the men's camp
To the left the women's camp
At the end of the ramp
right and left
the new crematoriums
numbered II and III
At the switch
the trains were usually
shunted onto the track to the right

COUNSEL FOR
THE DEFENSE: How long was the platform

8TH WITNESS: About 850 yards long

COUNSEL FOR
THE DEFENSE: How long were the trains

8TH WITNESS: They usually took up about two thirds
             of the platform

COUNSEL FOR
THE DEFENSE: Where were the selections carried out

8TH WITNESS: In the middle of the platform

COUNSEL FOR
THE DEFENSE: Where did the people line up

8TH WITNESS: At both ends of the platform

COUNSEL FOR
THE DEFENSE: How wide was the platform

8TH WITNESS: About 30 feet wide

COUNSEL FOR
THE DEFENSE: There the people stood
             in two groups next to each other
             each group lined up in rows of five
             We doubt very much that
             in that crowd
             the witness could have stood
             near the selecting officers
             for any amount of time

JUDGE: Accused Dr Frank
             did you take part
             in the selection procedure

ACCUSED #4: I was sometimes assigned
             to platform duty
             as a replacement
             My assignment was

to remove equipment
from arriving dentists
for use in the camp's dental station
I also registered the dentists
and dental technicians
and saw to it that they were issued clothing
When someone claimed to be a dentist
but in fact wasn't
I did not send him back
After all
we had to have somebody around
to clean up

JUDGE: Did you ever try
to have yourself released
from platform duty

ACCUSED #4: I reported to Dr Wirth at headquarters
for that very reason
The only answer given was
Camp duty is front-line duty
Any refusal
will be regarded as desertion
and dealt with accordingly

JUDGE: Did you escort
transports to the gas chambers

ACCUSED #4: No
Escort duty was the responsibility
of the guards
I myself did all I could
to help the prisoners
In my ward
I made their stay
as pleasant as possible

They could wear suits that fit
and they didn't have to shave their heads

JUDGE: Accused Dr Schatz
did you take part in the selections

ACCUSED #5: I never had anything to do with them
When I was ordered to the platform
to receive medicines
or medical instruments
I did all I could to get out of it
I came to the camp
under protest
I was ordered there
from an infantry dental station
Furthermore I would like to point out
that I enjoyed an unusually cordial
relationship with the prisoners

JUDGE: Accused Dr Lucas
what did you do on the platform

ACCUSED #6: I never did anything there at all
Time and again I said
My job as a doctor is to save lives
not destroy them
Also as a Catholic
I cannot take any other position
When attempts were made to force me I said
I was physically unable
I feigned various illnesses and tried
to get transferred back to the army
as soon as possible
I approached my old commanding officer
who said

I should do my best
to avoid making myself
unpleasantly conspicuous
Once on leave I even went so far
as to speak to an archbishop
a friend of mine
and to a prominent lawyer as well
Both told me
that illegal orders need not be obeyed
but that this should not be carried
to the extreme
where one's own life might be endangered
We were at war
and all sorts of things
were going on

PROSECUTING
ATTORNEY: Dr Lucas
               what kind of illnesses did you simulate
               when you were ordered to take part
               in the selections

ACCUSED #6:   I feigned biliary colic
               or some kind of stomach upset

PROSECUTING
ATTORNEY: Didn't anyone ever find it odd
               that your attacks of colic
               occurred only
               when you were assigned to platform duty

ACCUSED #6:   There was never any trouble
               Passive resistance
               was the only way
               for me to have as little to do
               with those things as possible
               I still don't see even now
               how else I could have acted then

PROSECUTING
ATTORNEY: And when you did have to participate
what did you do

ACCUSED #6: Only in three or four cases
my excuses didn't work
I was ordered
to the platform
under the threat
of being taken away then and there
if I did not obey
The meaning of the threat
was unmistakable

PROSECUTING
ATTORNEY: And then you took part in the selections

ACCUSED #6: All I had to do
was choose people who were fit for work
and the way I chose
many who were obviously unfit
also came into the camp

PROSECUTING
ATTORNEY: And the others

ACCUSED #6: They were led aside

PROSECUTING
ATTORNEY: When the selection was over
what happened to the luggage

8TH WITNESS: It was taken to the personal-effects camp
sorted there and stacked

PROSECUTING
ATTORNEY: How large was the personal-effects camp

8TH WITNESS: It consisted of 35 barracks

PROSECUTING
ATTORNEY: Could you estimate
the amount and value
of the goods seized

8TH WITNESS: Before deportation
the prisoners had been advised
to take with them
as many objects of value as possible
sheets clothing money and tools
The reason given was
that where they were going
they wouldn't be able to obtain anything
Thus
they brought every last thing
they could
Much had already been taken from them
on the platform
even before the selection began
The doctors in charge took
not only medical instruments
but also suitcases
full of currency and jewelry
Then the guards and the trainmen
took their share
For us
too
there was always something left over
which we could use to trade with
later on
Still when the final inventory
was drawn up in the personal-effects office
the total value amounted to millions

PROSECUTING
ATTORNEY: Could you give us any particulars
about the value of the goods
taken from the prisoners

8TH WITNESS: According to the final inventory
covering the period from April 1 1942
to December 15 1943
the value of the currency
stocks precious metals and jewels seized
amounted to 33 million dollars
In addition 1900 freight-car loads of textiles
valued at 12 million dollars
This does not include the final year
in which the biggest transports
were yet to come

PROSECUTING
ATTORNEY: Who received these assets

8TH WITNESS: The goods were forwarded
to the treasury
or in some cases to the Department of Finance

JUDGE: Were there ever any attempts at resistance
on the platform
The arrivals greatly outnumbered
the guards
They were being separated from their families
Their possessions were being taken from them
Did they not resist

9TH WITNESS: They did not resist

JUDGE: Why not

9TH WITNESS: The arrivals were starved
and exhausted
Their only desire was
to rest at last

JUDGE: Did they have no idea
                of what was in store for them

9TH WITNESS: How could they foresee
                that practically speaking
                they had ceased to exist
                Each one of them still believed
                he could survive

THE SONG OF THE CAMP

I

4TH WITNESS: When we had crossed the tracks
and were lined up
in front of the camp gate
I heard
a prisoner say to one of the women
That Red Cross truck takes gas
to the crematoriums
Your relatives will be killed there
The woman began to scream
An officer who had overheard the prisoner
turned to the woman
and said
But my dear woman
how can you believe
what a prisoner tells you
They're all either criminals
or insane
Look at the way their ears stick out
and their shaved heads
How can you listen to such people

JUDGE: Do you recall
who the officer was

4TH WITNESS: I saw him again later
I was his secretary
in the Political Section
His name is Broad

JUDGE: Can you point out
the accused Broad

4TH WITNESS: That is Mr Broad
[*The Accused Broad nods amiably
to the witness*]

JUDGE: What happened to the prisoner

4TH WITNESS: I heard
he was sentenced to 150 strokes
for spreading reports of atrocities
He died from it

JUDGE: Does the accused Broad
have anything to say to this

ACCUSED #16: I don't recall the case
But 150 strokes
We never ordered that many

3RD WITNESS: Even though our luggage was left behind
and we were separated
from our families
we still walked unsuspecting
through the gate between the barbed wire
We thought
our wives and children
were going to be fed on the other side
and that we would be allowed
to see them again soon
But then we saw
hundreds of ragged figures
many of them starved down to skeletons
We lost all hope

6TH WITNESS: One of them came up to us
and shouted
Prisoners
See that smoke behind the barracks
That smoke
is your wives and children
And for you too now that you're in here
there's only one way out
Up through the soot in the chimneys

3RD WITNESS: We were pushed into a washroom barrack
Guards and prisoners came
with stacks of papers
We had to strip
and everything we still had on us
was taken away
Watches rings papers pictures
were registered in personal files
Then numbers were tattooed
on the left forearm

JUDGE: How was this done

3RD WITNESS: The numbers were pricked into our skin
with a needle stamp
then ink was rubbed in
Our hair was cut off
and we had a cold shower
After that we got our clothes

JUDGE: What clothes were you given

3RD WITNESS: A pair of shorts full of holes
an undershirt
a torn jacket
a pair of patched pants

a cap
and a pair of wooden shoes
Then we set off at the double
to our barrack

JUDGE: What did your barrack look like

3RD WITNESS: A wooden barrack without windows
A door in the front and one in the back
Small skylights up under the roof
Right and left
three-decker bunks
the bottom level on the ground
the bunks supported by partition beams
Length of the barrack about 130 feet

JUDGE: How many prisoners
were quartered there

3RD WITNESS: It was built to hold 500 people
There were 1000 of us

JUDGE: How many such barracks were there

3RD WITNESS: More than 200

JUDGE: How wide were the bunks

3RD WITNESS: About six feet
Six men to a bunk
They had to keep shifting from
their right side over to their left

JUDGE: Was any bedding provided

3RD WITNESS: Some of the bunks had straw

The straw was rotten
and it sifted down from the top
onto the lower bunks
There was one blanket for each bunk
The men who lay on the outside
kept trying to pull the blanket
over their way
The strongest lay in the middle

JUDGE: Were the barracks heated

3RD WITNESS: There were two stoves
The stovepipes went into a chimney
in the middle of the barrack
They were bricked over
and the top of the brickwork
served as a table
The stoves were hardly ever heated

JUDGE: Were there sanitary installations
in the barracks

3RD WITNESS: There were wood troughs for washing
in the washroom barracks
A pipe with holes in it ran over the troughs
Water dripped out of the pipe
In the latrine there were long cement troughs
covered with boards with round holes in them
200 people could use them at one time
The latrine detail saw to it
that nobody sat there too long
They clubbed the prisoners right and left
to drive them out
Many of the prisoners
simply couldn't get done that quick
Part of their rectum stuck out from the strain

As soon as they had been driven out
of the latrine
they got back in line
There wasn't any paper
Many people tore pieces off their clothes
to wipe themselves with
or stole
pieces from each other's clothes at night
to have some in reserve
You had to relieve yourself in the morning
After that you couldn't
Anybody caught trying
was locked up
Water from the washroom barracks drained
into the latrine
to carry off the filth on the floor
The latrines kept getting stopped up
because the water pressure was too low
Then the shit detail came in
to pump it out
The stink from the latrines
mixed in with the smell
of the smoke

4TH WITNESS: The bowls we were given
served three different functions
to wash in
to get our supper in
and to relieve ourselves in at night
In the women's camp
the only place you could get water
was right next to the latrine
At that thin trickle of water
that ran off into the vats full of excrement
women stood and drank
and tried

to collect enough water in their bowls
so they could wash
Those who gave up washing
had given up

5TH WITNESS: Even as I jumped out of the freight car
into that confusion on the platform
I knew that what mattered here was
to look out for yourself
to try to work your way up
to make a good impression
and to keep away from anything
that might drag you down
When they made us lie down on the tables
in the reception room
and inspected our rectums
and our sexual organs
for concealed valuables
every last remnant
of our usual life
vanished
Family
home
occupation
and possessions
were ideas
that were wiped out
when the number
was stamped into your arm
And already we had started to live
with a new set of values
and to adjust to this world
which for anyone
who wanted to survive in it
became a normal world
The supreme commandment was

to stay healthy
and to show you were physically strong
I stuck close to those
who were too weak
to eat their rations
so I could take their food
at the first opportunity
I didn't take my eyes off
those who were dying
if they had a better sleeping place than I
Our way up in this new society
started in the barrack
which was our home now
From starting out sleeping
on the cold mud floor
we fought our way up
to the warm places on the top bunks
When two had to eat
out of the same bowl
they stared at each other's throats
to make sure
the other wasn't swallowing
an extra spoonful
It was normal
that everything had been stolen from us
It was normal
that we stole too
Dirt sores and diseases
were what was normal
It was normal
that all around us people were dying
and it was normal
to live in the face of one's own death
Our feelings grew numb
and we looked at corpses
with complete indifference

and that was normal
And it was normal
that there were some among us
who helped those who stood over us
to beat us
The woman who became
the Barrack-elder's maid
had come up in that world
and those who managed
to ingratiate themselves
with the Barrack-leader
rose even higher
Only the cunning survived
only those who every day
with unrelenting alertness
took and held their bit of ground
The unfit
the retarded
the slow
the gentle
the bewildered and the impractical
the ones who mourned and the ones
who pitied themselves
were crushed

6TH WITNESS: The first morning
we lined up for roll call
It was raining
We stood there for hours
Behind the barbed wire
on the other side of the platform
the women were being beaten
and shoved into trucks
They were naked and they screamed
at us
They wanted us to help them
and we couldn't help them

4TH WITNESS: I walked into a barrack
that was full of corpses
I saw
something move a little among the dead
It was a young girl
I pulled her out of the barrack
into the street
and asked
Who are you
How long have you been here
I don't know
she said
Why were you lying in there
with the dead
I asked
I can't be with the living any more
she said
She died that night

5TH WITNESS: We were sent out to dig graves
Many of the women collapsed
trying to shovel the mud out
We were up to our hips in water
The guards stood by looking on
They were very young
One of the women turned to the captain
Captain
she said
I can't work this hard any more
I'm pregnant
The guards laughed
and one of them pushed her
down with a shovel
and kept her under the water
until she drowned

7TH WITNESS: I heard

a guard talking through the barbed wire
to a nine-year-old boy
You know a lot for a boy your age
he said
The boy answered
I know that I know a lot
and I also know
I'm not going to learn any more
He was loaded into a truck
with a group
of about 90 children
When the children started
screaming and struggling
the boy yelled
Get in here
Get in the truck
Stop your crying
You saw the way
your parents and grandparents
went
Climb in
then you'll get to see them again
And as they were being driven off
I heard
him shout back to the guard
You won't be forgiven
anything

THE SONG OF THE CAMP

II

8TH WITNESS: In the morning we got
a pint of coffee substitute
and a fifth of an ounce of sugar
Some of us
still had a piece of dry bread
saved up from the night before
At noon we got soup
It was made out of scraps of potatoes
turnips and cabbage
a minimum of meat or fat
and a mealy nutrient
that gave the soup
its typical taste
Sometimes there were pieces of paper
or rags in the soup
Prisoners fought
to get not to the head of the line
but as near the end as they could
The top third of the soup
was water
Only toward the bottom
was there anything nourishing
In the evening after roll call
each of us got his piece of bread
from 10 to 12 ounces
and various supplements
about ¾ of an ounce of sausage
an ounce of margarine
or a teaspoonful of turnip jelly

On Friday we sometimes got
five or six potatoes
Often these extra rations
were cut in half
or weren't given out at all
because the camp personnel
from the guards on
up to the commanding officer
helped themselves
to the prisoners' food supply store
as much as they wanted

PROSECUTING
ATTORNEY: How many calories
did the daily rations contain

8TH WITNESS: About 1000 to 1300 calories
At rest
the body uses 1700
At hard labor
it requires about 4800
Since all the prisoners worked hard
their last reserves were quickly consumed
Movements grew progressively slower
according to the various stages of hunger
until there was no strength left
to keep the body in motion
Drowsiness and apathy
were characteristic symptoms
of weakness
Emaciation of the body
was accompanied by an exhaustion of mind
which terminated in a complete loss
of interest in all external events
In this condition
a prisoner could no longer
concentrate his thoughts

His memory was so greatly weakened
that frequently he could not
even remember his own name
On the average
a prisoner could not hold out
longer than three months

COUNSEL FOR
THE DEFENSE: How then did you
manage to survive

8TH WITNESS: Those who survived
were only those
who in the first few weeks managed
to get some kind of inside position
either because of their specialized skills
or by being assigned to special duties
in the camp work
A special-duty prisoner
who knew how to
exploit the privileges of his position
could obtain practically anything

COUNSEL FOR
THE DEFENSE: What privileged position did you hold

8TH WITNESS: I was a prisoner doctor
At first in the quarantine camp
Later in the infirmary

JUDGE: What were the conditions there

8TH WITNESS: In the quarantine camp there were rats
They bit not only the corpses
but also the critically ill
In the morning the feet of the dying
were often bleeding from rat bites
At night the rats took the bread

out of the prisoners' pockets
The prisoners frequently accused each other
You stole my bread
But it was the rats
Fleas infested the camp
by the million
Those who had boots got rid of them
because the fleas
made those precious possessions unbearable
With socks and rags
you could at least scratch
Conditions in the prisoners' infirmary
were better
There were crepe-paper bandages
cellulose
a keg of ichthyol ointment
and a barrel of talcum powder
All wounds were treated with the ointment
and barber's itch was covered with talcum
so it wouldn't show
We had a few tablets of aspirin
They were strung up on thread
Patients with fever under 100 degrees
were allowed one lick
Patients with fever over 100 degrees
could lick twice

JUDGE: What were the most common illnesses

8TH WITNESS: Aside from general weakness
                and bodily injuries caused by ill-treatment
                we had spotted fever and paratyphoid fever
                abdominal typhus erysipelas and tuberculosis
                as well as the characteristic camp disease
                incurable diarrhea
                Furunculosis flourished in the camp

Guards clubbed abscesses open
until the skin peeled off to the bone
In the camp I saw diseases
I never dreamed I would see
diseases
one only reads about in medical texts
There was Noma for instance
a disease that occurs
only in completely debilitated people
eating holes through the cheeks
until you can see
right through to the teeth
Or phemphicus
an extremely rare disease
which detaches the skin
in blisters
and after a few days
results in death

9TH WITNESS: After the evening roll call
the Barrack-elder
picked some of us out for exercise
We had to hop like frogs
He kept shouting
Jump faster faster
and if somebody didn't keep up
he pounded them with a footstool
until they collapsed

JUDGE: What was this Barrack-elder's name

9TH WITNESS: His name was Bednarek
I can point him out

ACCUSED #18: I never heard of anybody being beaten
during the exercise period

JUDGE: What did take place
                during the exercise period

ACCUSED #18:Prisoners who attracted attention
                had to do some light exercises
                To the left
                To the right
                That was all

9TH WITNESS: In winter Bednarek made
                prisoners stand under the cold shower
                for half an hour
                until they were numb with cold
                Then they were thrown out into the yard
                where they died

ACCUSED #18:These accusations are simply made up
                I couldn't possibly
                have done that sort of thing
                I was a special-duty prisoner myself
                I had the Kapo over me
                the work supervisor
                and the camp-elder
                I myself
                and I can say it with pride today
                let prisoners sleep in my room
                and in our block after supper
                we always had a good time

9TH WITNESS: After Bednarek
                had beaten a prisoner to death
                he went into his room
                and prayed

ACCUSED #18:It's true
                I'm a religious man

But as for praying I didn't dare
There were too many informers for that
And I never killed anybody
At the most
there was maybe a slap now and then
when I had to break up an argument

3RD WITNESS: More than any of the others
there was one who was first
when it came to beating or killing
His name was Kaduk
Kaduk we all knew what that name meant

JUDGE: Could the witness
point out the accused Kaduk

3RD WITNESS: That is Mr Kaduk
[*The Accused grins at the witness*]
The prisoners called him
Professor
or
the Holy Doctor Kaduk
because he carried out
selections on his own
With the crook of his walking stick
he fished out his victims
by the neck or leg

ACCUSED #7: Mr Chairman
that statement is not true

3RD WITNESS: I was there
when Kaduk had hundreds of prisoners
hauled out of the hospital
They had to strip in the laundry barrack
and then run past Kaduk

in single file
He held his walking stick out
about a yard off the ground
in front of him
They had to jump over it
If they touched the stick
they were taken off to be gassed
If they cleared it without touching it
they were beaten until they collapsed
Now try it again
Kaduk shouted
But the second time
nobody cleared it

ACCUSED #7: I selected no prisoners
I made no decisions
I had no such authority

JUDGE: What was within your authority

ACCUSED #7: I had to be on hand
during the selections
I watched like a hawk
to make sure nobody
from the selected group slipped over
into the work-fit group

JUDGE: Did you have any other duties
on the platform

ACCUSED #7: Yes
I had to organize
the group traffic

JUDGE: How did you do that

ACCUSED #7: Everybody out
Baggage on the platform
Fall in columns of five
Forward march

3RD WITNESS: Kaduk fired
at random
into the crowd

ACCUSED #7: I never even thought of
firing at random
If I had wanted to shoot
I would have hit
whoever I was aiming at
I was strict
I'll admit that
But I only did
what I had to do

JUDGE: And what did you have to do

ACCUSED #7: Make sure that the operation ran smoothly
It was regulations that children
were immediately set aside
also mothers who didn't want
to be separated from their children
Everything went without a hitch
The transports rolled in
like a line of sausages
There wasn't any need to rough anybody up
They all took it very well
They didn't resist
since they could see
resistance would have been pointless

6TH WITNESS: Once Kaduk hit one of the prisoners

in our work detail
knocked him down
then laid his walking stick
down across his throat
put one foot on each end of the stick
and rocked from side to side
until the man choked to death

ACCUSED #7: Lies
Lies

JUDGE: Sit down Kaduk
You will not shout at the witness

ACCUSED #7: Mr Chairman
What he says there
simply isn't true
All I care about here is the truth
No prisoner was ever killed
that way in our camp
We had orders
to go easy
with the work force
Sometimes though I'd only lift my hand
and somebody would fall over
pretending he had fainted
    [*The Accused laugh*]
Mr Chairman
we weren't interested in beating anybody
We were on our feet
from 5:30 in the morning
and then at night we
still had to go on platform duty
That was enough for us
Mr Chairman
all I want is to live in peace

These last years have proved that
I was a hospital attendant
and my patients loved me
They can bear me out on that
Papa Kaduk
that's what they called me
Doesn't that tell the whole story
Why should I have to pay now
for what I had to do then
Everybody else did it too
So why of all people
did they arrest me

THE SONG OF THE CAMP

III

4TH WITNESS: The more you managed to push down
whoever was under you
the more secure your own position was
I could see the whole face
of our Barrack-elder change
when she talked to a superior
She was cheerful and friendly then
and behind that you could feel her fear
Sometimes her supervisor
treated her like her best friend
and she enjoyed many privileges
But if the supervisor
had had a bad night just once
then she would be done for
from one minute to the next
And she had already been through everything
she had seen her relatives shot down
she had been forced to watch
as they murdered her children
she had grown completely numb
like the rest of us
She knew
that once she went under
nobody would help her
and whoever took over
would go on beating
so she beat us
because she wanted
to stay on top at any price

5TH WITNESS: The question
of right and wrong
didn't exist any longer
The only thing that counted
was what was immediately useful
Only our masters could afford
to have moods
and even to show how moved they were
or to be sympathetic
and make plans for the future
The camp doctor Dr Rohde
let me work in his ward
He found out
we had gone to school in the same city
and asked me
if we hadn't perhaps met each other
at the Ritter
where he frequently stopped in
for a glass of wine
and I thought
Fine if that's the way you want it
I'll go along with you
and so I reminded him of his youth
and he said
After the war we'll meet there again
for a glass of wine
Dr Mengele sent flowers to a pregnant woman
and the wife of the camp commander
sent her best regards
and a baby sweater she had knitted herself
to the children's barrack
where somebody had thought
it would be a nice idea
to paint dwarfs on the walls
and set up a sandbox
The paths to the crematoriums

were carefully raked after each batch
of prisoners had gone by
The bushes along the way were trimmed
and flower beds had been planted
in the grass that grew
over the underground chambers
Mengele used to arrive smartly dressed
his thumbs stuck in his belt
He would nod pleasantly to the children
who called him Uncle
before they were cut up in his laboratory
But there was another man I remember
His name was Flacke
Nobody starved to death in his ward
and the prisoners there all wore
clean clothes
I asked him once
Sir who are you doing this for
Someday
we will all have to be done away with
because not a single witness
can be left behind
He said
there will be enough of us here
who will find a way to prevent that

PROSECUTING
ATTORNEY: Do you mean to say
                that each one of the men in charge
                could take a stand
                against conditions in the camp
                and change them

5TH WITNESS: That is exactly what I was trying to say

1ST WITNESS: Normal reactions
             were possible only in the first few hours

58

After one had been there for a time
it was impossible
Once you fell into the routine
you were caught
and had to cooperate

PROSECUTING
ATTORNEY: As a doctor
you were assigned to prevent
the spread of epidemics

1ST WITNESS: Cases of spotted and typhoid fever
had broken out among some
of the camp personnel and their families
I was ordered
by the Health Institute
to report to the camp

PROSECUTING
ATTORNEY: Then your presence there had nothing to do
with treating the prisoners themselves

1ST WITNESS: No
PROSECUTING
ATTORNEY: Did you get an impression
of conditions in the camp

1ST WITNESS: Shortly after I arrived
the doctor in charge of the laboratory said
I realize this is all new to you
but it's not half so bad
We don't have anything to do
with the liquidation program here
and it's none of our business either
If after two weeks
you decide you don't want to stay here
you can leave
With the intention to leave the camp

after two weeks
I went to work
A few days later
the chief camp doctor Dr Wirth
ordered me to take part
in the selections on the platform
When I told him
I don't want to have anything to do
with that
he said
You won't have much to do there
But I still refused

PROSECUTING
ATTORNEY: What happened when you refused

1ST WITNESS: Nothing
I didn't have to take part
in the selections

PROSECUTING
ATTORNEY: Did you leave the camp
after your first two weeks

1ST WITNESS: No
I decided to stay after all
and see if I couldn't do something
about the contagious diseases
I felt that I could
at least in a few cases
prevent things
without exposing myself
As a result of my work the threat
of the epidemic was ended

PROSECUTING
ATTORNEY: Among the camp personnel that is
Not among the prisoners

1ST WITNESS: Yes
That was my assignment

JUDGE: You were at that time in charge
of the sentry units both within
and outside the camp
also of the guard units
attached to the work details
What did that involve

2ND WITNESS: My assignment was
to keep an eye on the guards
to see they carried out their charge
diligently and faithfully

JUDGE: What regulations were they under

2ND WITNESS: When a prisoner tried to escape
the guard was required to call out three times
before firing a warning shot
If the prisoner still didn't halt
he was to be shot
to prevent further flight

JUDGE: Were any prisoners shot
for this reason

2ND WITNESS: Not under my command

JUDGE: Did prisoners
run up against the electrically charged
barbed wires

2ND WITNESS: Not under my command

JUDGE: Did it ever occur

2ND WITNESS: I heard it happened sometimes

JUDGE: Did guard details
obey regulations

2ND WITNESS: As far as I know
Yes
On my word of honor

JUDGE: Do you know anything about cap shooting

2ND WITNESS: About what

JUDGE: Shooting caps

2ND WITNESS: I've heard about it

JUDGE: What did you hear

2ND WITNESS: They said
caps were thrown up
and then they shot at them

JUDGE: Who threw the caps
whose caps
and who did the shooting

2ND WITNESS: That I don't know

JUDGE: What were you told then

2ND WITNESS: Yes
Well
A prisoner was ordered
to take off his cap
and throw it away

and then
Move
run and get your cap they'd say
and when he started to run
they'd shoot him down

JUDGE: And if he didn't run

2ND WITNESS: Then they'd shoot him too
                  because that was refusal to obey an order
PROSECUTING
ATTORNEY: Were special rations
                  or special leaves granted
                  as a reward for
                  shooting prisoners attempting escape

2ND WITNESS: I never heard of that happening
                  I don't believe it either
                  To be rewarded for such behavior
                  would degrade a soldier's reputation
PROSECUTING
ATTORNEY: The court has in its possession
                  documents which show
                  that in a number of instances
                  sentries were rewarded for
                  shooting prisoners attempting escape
                  Furthermore lists of prisoners
                  shot while attempting escape
                  were posted and periodically
                  brought up to date

2ND WITNESS: That's news to me
PROSECUTING
ATTORNEY: According to our information
                  you are currently
                  director of an insurance company

COUNSEL FOR
THE DEFENSE: We object to
these irrelevant interjections
by the prosecution

PROSECUTING
ATTORNEY: We take it for granted
that the witness
realizes the significance
of a signature

2ND WITNESS: Certainly

PROSECUTING
ATTORNEY: Some of these lists
bear your signature

2ND WITNESS: It's possible
that on some occasion
I had to sign as a matter of routine
I can't remember

THE SONG OF THE SWING

I

JUDGE: As a prisoner
you were employed
in the Political Division
What did you do there

5TH WITNESS: At first I was stenographer and typist
in the administrative office
then because of my knowledge of languages
I was made interpreter

JUDGE: Who assigned you to this position

5TH WITNESS: Mr Boger

JUDGE: Do you recognize
Boger among the accused

5TH WITNESS: That is Mr Boger
    [*The accused Boger
    greets the witness amiably*]

COUNSEL FOR
THE DEFENSE: Where precisely
was the Political Division located

5TH WITNESS: It was a wooden barrack
directly behind the entrance

COUNSEL FOR
THE DEFENSE: Behind which entrance

5TH WITNESS: Just to the left behind the entrance
to the old camp

COUNSEL FOR
THE DEFENSE: How far was the old camp
from the main camp

5TH WITNESS: About two miles

COUNSEL FOR
THE DEFENSE: Where were your living quarters

5TH WITNESS: In the women's camp

COUNSEL FOR
THE DEFENSE: Could you describe for us
the way you took to your office

5TH WITNESS: We had to leave camp
every morning
and walk along the side of the fields
The road crossed the tracks
where the switch engines
shunted the freight cars
We frequently had to wait at the barrier
On the other side of the tracks
there were more fields
and a couple of empty farmhouses
Then we went through a barred gate
There were trees
and the old crematorium
Next to it was the Political Division

COUNSEL FOR
THE DEFENSE: Was the Political Division
within the camp proper

5TH WITNESS: It was outside the camp
First
there were the administration buildings

Then the two barbed-wire fences
and the observation towers
Behind that were the barracks
where the prisoners lived

COUNSEL FOR
THE DEFENSE: What did the Political Division barrack
look like

5TH WITNESS: It was one story high
and painted green

COUNSEL FOR
THE DEFENSE: What did the administrative office look like

5TH WITNESS: There were flower pots on the window sills
and there were curtains
and on the walls
pictures and mottoes

COUNSEL FOR
THE DEFENSE: What kind of pictures and mottoes

5TH WITNESS: I can't remember any more

COUNSEL FOR
THE DEFENSE: Who supervised the work in the office

5TH WITNESS: Mr Broad
We typists always had
to look our best
We were allowed to let our hair grow
We wore kerchiefs
and civilian clothes and shoes
We spat on our shoes in the morning
and polished them with our hands

COUNSEL FOR
THE DEFENSE: How did Mr Boger treat you

5TH WITNESS: Mr Boger always treated me decently

Frequently he gave me his mess kit
with the leftovers
He saved my life once
when I was about to be transferred
to a penal company
A Kapo had reported me
for doing a careless job of dusting
Mr Boger revoked the sentence

JUDGE: How many typists worked
              in the Political Division

5TH WITNESS: We were 16 girls

JUDGE: What did you have to do

5TH WITNESS: We had to keep the death lists up to date
              We had to enter the particulars
              relating to date and cause of death
              This was called the Discharge
              Mr Broad grew furious
              if he found a single mistake in our typing

JUDGE: How was the filing organized

5TH WITNESS: There were two tables
              On one table
              were the card-index boxes
              with the numbers of the living
              On the other the boxes
              with the numbers of the dead
              By looking at these we could see
              how many from a given shipment
              were still alive

Out of a 100 after a week
there were two dozen

JUDGE: Were all deaths
                that occurred within the camp
                recorded there

5TH WITNESS: Only prisoners
                who had received a number
                were kept on the books
                Those who were taken directly
                from the platform to the gas
                were not entered on any list

JUDGE: What were the causes of death
                that you entered

5TH WITNESS: Most of them
                were fictitious
                For instance we were not allowed to write
                Shot while attempting escape
                but had to write heart attack instead
                Instead of malnutrition we wrote
                dysentery
                We had to make sure
                no two prisoners died at the same minute
                and that the cause of death
                corresponded to their age
                Therefore no 20-year-old could die
                of a weak heart
                In the beginning letters were still sent
                to the next of kin

PROSECUTING
ATTORNEY: Can you recall the text of these letters

5TH WITNESS: In spite of all medical treatment

69

It has unfortunately been impossible
to save the life of the detained
We extend our deepest sympathies
to you for this great loss
At your request the urn
will be sent to you
COD at a cost of three dollars

PROSECUTING
ATTORNEY: Were the ashes of the deceased
actually in these urns

5TH WITNESS: The ashes of many dead
were in those urns
We could see out of the windows
the dead piled up
in front of the old crematorium
They were dumped there by the truckload

PROSECUTING
ATTORNEY: Could you give us an idea
of the number of the dead
entered in your office

5TH WITNESS: We worked 12 to 15 hours a day
on the official books of the dead
It came to about 300 dead per day

PROSECUTING
ATTORNEY: Were any of those deaths
caused directly
by the Political Division

5TH WITNESS: Prisoners died there daily
either by mistreatment or execution

COUNSEL FOR
THE DEFENSE: Where were the prisoners executed

5TH WITNESS: In the camp in Barrack 11

COUNSEL FOR THE DEFENSE:	Were you allowed to enter the camp
5TH WITNESS:	No but we knew of everything that went on Every memorandum and report related to the camp passed through our office Boger said to us What you hear and see here you have neither heard nor seen
JUDGE:	How were the interrogations in the Political Division carried out
5TH WITNESS:	Boger always began very calmly He came up close to the prisoner and asked the questions that I had to interpret If the prisoner didn't answer he shook a bunch of keys in front of the man's face If the prisoner still didn't answer Boger hit him in the face with the keys Then he went up even closer and said I have a machine that will make you talk
JUDGE:	What sort of machine was this
5TH WITNESS:	Boger called it his talking machine
JUDGE:	Where was it
5TH WITNESS:	In the next room

JUDGE:	Did you ever see the machine

5TH WITNESS:	Yes

JUDGE:	What did it look like

5TH WITNESS:	It was made out of poles

COUNSEL FOR THE DEFENSE:	Are you sure you remember this correctly

5TH WITNESS:	It was a frame They were hung on it We heard the beating and the screaming After an hour or after several hours they were carried out They were unrecognizable

JUDGE:	Were they still alive

5TH WITNESS:	If they weren't dead then they seldom lived much longer Once Boger saw me crying He said This is no place for personal feelings

JUDGE:	For what reasons were prisoners subjected to such punishment

5TH WITNESS:	Sometimes it was because somebody had stolen a piece of bread or because he was too slow in responding to an order to work faster Frequently it was enough that an informer

had denounced somebody
There was an informer's box
Anybody could drop a note in

ACCUSED #2: I had nothing to do
with that kind of nonsense
In the Political Division we dealt
exclusively with resistance problems
within the camp

JUDGE: How often did the witness herself see
prisoners die
after being taken down from the machine

5TH WITNESS: At least 20 times

JUDGE: You can vouch for the fact
that in at least 20 cases
prisoners died in your presence

5TH WITNESS: Yes

JUDGE: Did you ever see
the punishment being carried out

5TH WITNESS: Yes
I saw a man hanging there once
with his head down
Another time a woman was
strapped up on the poles
Boger forced us
to go in and look

ACCUSED #2: It is true
that the witness was an interpreter
However she was never present

at any of the intensive interrogations
On such occasions
ladies were never permitted

5TH WITNESS: Ladies

ACCUSED #2: I think I can say that now
                [*The Accused laugh*]

JUDGE: Did the witness
see any of the accused present
take part in the beatings

5TH WITNESS: I saw Boger in his shirt sleeves
holding his whip
and I often saw him
come out spattered with blood
Once I heard Broad say to Lachmann
another member of the Political Division
You know Gerhard
he spouted blood like a pig
Then he handed me his coat
to clean
They always made a big point
of cleanliness
Broad liked to look at himself in the mirror
looking very pleased
especially after he was promoted
to private first class
and I had sewed
his stripe on for him
I had to clean Boger's boots once

JUDGE: Yes

5TH WITNESS: A truckload of children
drove by outside
I saw it through the office window
A small boy jumped off the truck
He was holding an apple
Boger came out the door
The child stood there with his apple
Boger went over to the child
grabbed him by the ankles
and smashed his head
against the barrack wall
Then he picked up the apple
called me out and said
Wipe that off the wall
Later at an interrogation
I saw him eat the apple

COUNSEL FOR
THE DEFENSE: You made no mention of this
at the preliminary hearings

5TH WITNESS: I couldn't speak about it

COUNSEL FOR
THE DEFENSE: Why not

5TH WITNESS: For personal reasons

COUNSEL FOR
THE DEFENSE: Could you tell us
what those reasons are

5TH WITNESS: Since that time
I have never wanted to have
a child of my own

COUNSEL FOR
THE DEFENSE: How is it
that you can speak about it now

5TH WITNESS: Now that I see him again
            I must speak

JUDGE: What does the accused Boger
            have to say in reply
            to these accusations

ACCUSED #2: They are completely made up
            a poor way for the witness to repay me
            for the trust
            I placed in her in those days

THE SONG OF THE SWING

II

7TH WITNESS: I was brought into the interrogation room
of the Political Division
together with some other prisoners

JUDGE: Can you describe this room

7TH WITNESS: There were expensive rugs on the floor
that had come off
one of the transports from France
Boger's desk
was set at an angle across from the door
He was sitting on the desk when I came in
The interpreter sat behind the desk

JUDGE: Who else was present in the room

7TH WITNESS: The head of the Political Division
Grabner
and the accused Dylewski and Broad

JUDGE: What did they say

7TH WITNESS: Boger said
We are the Political Division
We don't ask questions
We listen
You ought to know what you have to say

JUDGE: Why had you been brought there

7TH WITNESS: I didn't know
I didn't know what
I was supposed to say
and I asked them to question me
I was beaten senseless
When I came to I was lying in the hall
Boger was standing there
He said
Get up
But I couldn't get up
He came toward me
I pulled myself up against the wall
I saw I was bleeding
The floor and my clothes
were covered with blood
My head was split open
My nose was broken
All that afternoon and most of the night
I had to stand with my face to the wall
There were several others standing there
Anybody who turned
had his head knocked against the wall
The next day I was interrogated again
I was brought into the room
with the other prisoners

JUDGE: What did they want to find out

7TH WITNESS: The whole time I didn't know
what it was all about
A couple of times they
put something around my head
some kind of metal band I think
Then I was taken back to the hall
and Boger took the man next to me
into the room
His name was Walter Windmuller

JUDGE: Do you know what happened to him

7TH WITNESS: He was in there for about
                two or three hours
                I stood in the hallway
                with my face to the wall
                Then Windmuller came out
                He had to stand next to me
                Blood was running down his legs
                He fell over several times
                We had learned
                how to talk without moving our lips
                When I asked him what had happened
                he said
                They smashed my balls in there
                He died the same day

JUDGE: Was Boger responsible
                for this prisoner's death

7TH WITNESS: I am convinced that
                if Boger didn't do the killing himself
                he certainly helped kill him

JUDGE: Does the accused Boger
                have anything to say

ACCUSED #2:   Mr Chairman
                if I may be allowed to explain
                that's not the way it happened

JUDGE: How did it happen

ACCUSED #2:   Mr Chairman
                I didn't kill anybody
                I just had to carry out my interrogations

JUDGE: What kind of interrogations were they

ACCUSED #2: Occasionally
                  they were intensive interrogations
                  conducted
                  according to standard operating procedures

JUDGE: What was the reason for these procedures

ACCUSED #2: In the interest of camp security
                  it was essential
                  to take vigorous measures
                  against traitors and other harmful elements

JUDGE: Accused Boger
                  as a criminal investigator
                  didn't you know
                  that a man
                  subjected to such an interrogation
                  will say anything you want him to say

ACCUSED #2: That's not the way I see it at all
                  and especially not in view of
                  our specific task
                  If a prisoner proved stubborn
                  force was the only way
                  to make him confess

8TH WITNESS: When I was called into Boger's room
                  I saw
                  a plateful of herrings on his desk
                  Grabner asked me if I was hungry
                  I said no
                  But Grabner said
                  I know how long it's been
                  since you've eaten

Today you're going to see
how nice I can be
I'm going to give you something to eat
Boger's made a salad for you
He ordered me to eat
I couldn't
because my hands were handcuffed
behind my back
Then Boger pushed my face into the plate
I had to eat the herrings
They were so salty that I threw up
I had to lick up
the vomit together with the herrings
I still had some in my mouth
and Boger shouted
Watch him to make sure he doesn't
spit any of it out in the hall
Then they took me to Barrack 11
and up to the loft
My hands were tied behind me
I was hung from a pole by my hands
That was called pole-hanging
They hung you up just high enough
so that the bottom of your feet
barely touched the floor
Boger pushed me back and forth
and kicked me in the stomach
There was a pail of water in front of me
Boger asked me if I wanted to drink
He laughed and twisted me
one way and then the other
When I lost consciousness
they threw water over me
My arms grew numb
My wrists almost snapped
Boger questioned me

but my tongue was so swollen
I couldn't speak
Then Boger said
We still have another swing for you
I was
taken back to the Political Division

COUNSEL FOR
THE DEFENSE: Were you subjected to a session
on that swing too

8TH WITNESS: Yes
COUNSEL FOR
THE DEFENSE: Then it was possible
to survive it after all

THE SONG OF THE SWING

III

8TH WITNESS: I remember one morning
in the spring of 1942
A platoon of prisoner police
marched up in front of the barrack
of the former post office
where the Political Division
had been installed
At the head of the column were prisoners
carrying two wooden supports
built like the sides of a hurdle
Behind them were guards
armed with submachine guns
and behind them
the heads of the Political Division
They had their briefcases
and especially prepared dried-out bullwhips
that they used for corporal punishment
Those supports
were the frame for the new swing

JUDGE: Was that the first time
the apparatus was used

8TH WITNESS: It had existed before
in a simpler form
At first it was just a pipe
laid across two tables
and the prisoner was strapped to the pipe
Since the pipe turned when the prisoner

was beaten
this new frame was made to keep it stable

COUNSEL FOR
THE DEFENSE: Would the witness
tell us how he happens to know this

8TH WITNESS: Nothing happened in our part of the camp
that we didn't know about
In the old camp everything took place
at close quarters
The whole camp wasn't more than
about 200 yards wide and 300 long
From any one of the 28 barracks
you could see the whole camp

JUDGE: What was the reason for your being
brought in for interrogation

8TH WITNESS: I was assigned to the work detail
that put in the drainage ditch
around the outside of the camp
On the job I helped a fellow prisoner
get together with his mother
who was in the women's camp
The prisoner's name was Janicki
They took him
into the interrogation room first
When they were done with him
they threw him out into the hall
He was still alive
He opened his mouth
and stuck out his tongue as far as he could
He started to lick the floor
he was so thirsty
Boger came up and turned his head
with the toe of his boot

Then he said
It's your turn now
If you don't tell us the truth
the same thing will happen to you
Then they strapped me up on the swing

JUDGE: Would you
describe the procedure

8TH WITNESS: First the prisoner had
to sit down on the floor
and draw up his knees
His hands were tied in front
and then pushed down over his knees
Then they shoved the pipe in the space
between the arms and knees
Then the pipe was raised
and set into the wood frame

JUDGE: Who took care of these preparations

8TH WITNESS: Two special-duty prisoners

JUDGE: Who else was in the room

8TH WITNESS: I saw Boger there
and Broad and Dylewski
Boger asked the questions
but I couldn't answer
I hung with my head down
and the two special-duty prisoners
swung me back and forth

COUNSEL FOR
THE DEFENSE: What questions were you asked

8TH WITNESS: They asked me for more names

JUDGE:	Were you beaten during the questioning
8TH WITNESS:	Boger and Dylewski took turns with the bullwhip
COUNSEL FOR THE DEFENSE:	Wasn't it the prisoners who did the beating
8TH WITNESS:	I saw Boger and Dylewski with the whips in their hands
JUDGE:	Where did they beat you
8TH WITNESS:	On the buttocks back legs hands feet and the back of the head But they concentrated on the sexual organs They especially aimed for them I lost consciousness three times and they poured water on me
JUDGE:	Accused Boger do you admit to having mistreated this witness
ACCUSED #2:	There is only one answer to that a loud and definite no
8TH WITNESS:	I still have the scars from it
ACCUSED #2:	But not from me
JUDGE:	In the course of your interrogation did you ever make use of the instrument here described

ACCUSED #2: There were times
when I had to arrange for its use
The punishment
was carried out by special-duty prisoners
under my supervision

JUDGE: Do you regard
the witness' description
as untruthful

ACCUSED #2: The description leaves out a great deal
and in many respects fails
to conform to the truth

JUDGE: What was the truth

ACCUSED #2: The moment the prisoner confessed
punishment was discontinued

JUDGE: And if the prisoner did not confess

ACCUSED #2: He was beaten until he bled
That was it

JUDGE: Was a doctor present

ACCUSED #2: I never saw an order
requiring the presence of a doctor
nor was it necessary
because the instant blood began to flow
I stopped
The purpose of the intensive interrogation
was achieved
when blood ran down their pants

JUDGE: You felt you were fully justified

in carrying out these
intensive interrogations

ACCUSED #2: They were clearly in line
with the duties and responsibilities
of my command
What's more it is my opinion
that even now corporal punishment
if administered
by juvenile courts for instance
would soon put a stop to a good deal
of delinquent behavior

COUNSEL FOR
THE DEFENSE: It has been stated by the witness
that no one could survive
the swing
From all appearances
this claim would seem to be exaggerated

8TH WITNESS: When they took me down from the swing
Boger said
Now we've got you in shape
for a very pleasant heavenly ascension
I was taken to a cell in Barrack 11
I expected to be shot
at any time
I don't know
how many days I spent in there
The sores on my buttocks were festering
my testicles were blue and green
and tremendously swollen
Most of the time I was unconscious
Then I was taken to the washroom
with a number of other prisoners
We were told to strip
and our numbers were written

on our chests
with indelible ink
I knew that this
meant the death sentence
While we were standing there naked
the chief clerk came in and asked
how many prisoners should be crossed out
as executed
When he had left we were
recounted
There was one too many
I had learned always to be the last in line
Somebody kicked me
and I got my clothes back
I was to be taken back to the cell
to wait until the bunker was emptied again
but a prisoner orderly
took me with him to the infirmary
Sometimes
one of us did survive
and I
am one of those few who did

THE SONG OF THE POSSIBILITY
OF SURVIVAL

I

3RD WITNESS: The mood of the camp changed
from one day to the next
It depended on the mood
of the commanding officer
the adjutant
and the Barrack-leader
and it depended
on how the war was going at the time
At the beginning
when they were still winning
we were shoved around treated with contempt
but they could still joke when they hit us
But as the number of retreats
and defeats mounted
camp operations were stepped up
Still you never knew
what was going to happen
An order to fall out could mean anything
standing there for nothing
or getting harassed
In the infirmary
prisoners could get treatment until
they were well again and even
be put on a special diet
only to be sent up through the chimney
as soon as they had recovered
One of the prisoner orderlies was
beaten up by the camp doctor

because he had left out some minor detail
from a patient's chart
Meanwhile
the patient had already been killed
It was only by accident
that I
escaped the gassing
The ovens happened to be stopped up
that night
On the way back from the crematorium
the doctor who accompanied us found out
I was a medical student
and he found a place for me in his ward

JUDGE: What was this doctor's name

3RD WITNESS: Dr Vetter
He was a very well-bred man
Dr Schatz and Dr Frank
were also friendly to the prisoners
they delivered up to be killed
They did not kill out of hatred
or conviction
They killed only because they had to
and there was no point in discussing that
Only a few killed with passion
Boger was one of them
I saw prisoners
when they were called into Boger's room
and I saw them
when they came out
And when they were taken out to be shot
I heard Boger say with pride
These are mine
One prisoner who had been shot
was taken to the hospital

with an order from Boger
That man's life must be saved
so he can be hung
But the prisoner died in the hospital

JUDGE: Does the accused Boger
recall this case

ACCUSED #2: It was standard procedure that
prisoners wounded while attempting escape
were taken to the hospital
so they could be interrogated
when they had recovered
To that extent the witness' statement can
be considered absolutely correct
In this case I passed on the order
that the prisoner should be kept alive
I said
He must be saved
so he can be interrogated

JUDGE: Was he to be hanged after that

ACCUSED #2: That's possible
but that was not within my jurisdiction

6TH WITNESS: Boger and Kaduk
carried out hangings on their own
Once 12 prisoners were
to be executed
as a reprisal for the escape of a prisoner
Boger and Kaduk
put the noose
over the prisoners' heads

COUNSEL FOR
THE DEFENSE: How do you know that

6TH WITNESS: We stood on the assembly ground
We were ordered to watch
The prisoners shouted something
Boger and Kaduk went wild with rage
They started to kick
and slap them
then they hung on the prisoners' legs
and pulled them down

ACCUSED #2: All I recall of this incident
is that one of the sentenced
broke away
while he was being taken out
under strict guard
to be executed
He lunged at me
so hard he broke one of my ribs
He was overpowered
He was bound
and I read the sentence

JUDGE: Did the witness
hear the reading of a sentence

6TH WITNESS: No sentence was read

ACCUSED #2: Of course it was hard to hear the sentence
because the prisoners were shouting

PROSECUTING
ATTORNEY: What were they shouting

ACCUSED #2: Political slogans

PROSECUTING
ATTORNEY: Of what kind

ACCUSED #2: They were inciting the prisoners against us

93

COUNSEL FOR
THE DEFENSE: How did the prisoners react

ACCUSED #2: There were no observable incidents
The sentence was executed
as were all sentences
I did not carry out
the execution myself
That was done by special-duty Kapos

COUNSEL FOR
THE DEFENSE: Isn't it possible
that the witness simply failed to hear
the reading of the sentence

6TH WITNESS: The execution took place
immediately after the escape
There was no time
for the case to be considered
by a central office
and for a sentence to be handed down

JUDGE: Was the commanding officer
or his adjutant present

6TH WITNESS: Ranking officers were always present
at public executions
They wore white gloves
on such occasions
I can't say definitely
whether the adjutant was present
Still it can be taken for granted
since he was responsible
for the execution of all orders
within this area of command

JUDGE: Does the witness

94

recognize the adjutant
among the accused

6TH WITNESS: That one is Mulka

JUDGE: Accused Mulka
were you
present at this or any other hanging

ACCUSED #1: I had nothing to do
with any killing
of any kind

JUDGE: Did you hear of the orders in question
or did you ever pass such orders on

ACCUSED #1: I did hear of such orders
but I personally never passed them on

JUDGE: When faced with such orders
what did you do

ACCUSED #1: I was careful
not to trouble my superiors
with questions about the legality
of prisoner executions
that were brought to my attention
Ultimately of course
I had a responsibility
to my family
and to myself

PROSECUTING
ATTORNEY: Accused Mulka
did you ever see the gallows

ACCUSED #1: I beg your pardon

PROSECUTING
ATTORNEY: I asked whether you ever saw the gallows

ACCUSED #1:   No
                 I never set foot in the camp

PROSECUTING
ATTORNEY: You mean to say
                 that you
                 as adjutant to the commanding officer
                 were never in the camp

ACCUSED #1:   That's the absolute truth
                 The nature of my work was exclusively
                 administrative
                 I stayed strictly
                 within the administrative-office area

PROSECUTING
ATTORNEY: Where was this

ACCUSED #1:   In the army barracks
                 outside of the camp proper

PROSECUTING
ATTORNEY: Couldn't you see
                 into the camp from there

ACCUSED #1:   I don't believe you could

PROSECUTING
ATTORNEY: Could the witness
                 give us an idea of how the outer buildings
                 were situated in relation to the camp

6TH WITNESS: All the back windows
                 in the administrative buildings
                 looked out onto the camp
                 Directly behind the administration buildings
                 were the concrete posts

                              with the electrically charged barbed wire
                              10 yards from the posts was the first barrack
                              Right behind that one
                              the other barracks in three rows
                              The three rows 10 yards apart at the most
                              The view up the long streets
                              was unobstructed

PROSECUTING
ATTORNEY: Where were the gallows

6TH WITNESS: On the assembly ground
                              in front of the camp kitchen
                              Just to the right
                              as you come in through the main gate
                              onto the main street

PROSECUTING
ATTORNEY: Would you describe the gallows

6TH WITNESS: Three poles
                              with an iron rail across the top

PROSECUTING
ATTORNEY: Accused Mulka
                              you lived in close proximity to the camp
                              According to camp regulations
                              your position entailed
                              reporting to the commanding officer
                              all important events within the camp
                              and processing all coded material
                              as well as instructing all guard units
                              as to the larger significance
                              of their assignment
                              Holding such a position
                              were you not aware of the punishments
                              carried out in the camp

ACCUSED #1:   Only once did I see

                        some sort of signed and dated order
                        authorizing corporal punishment

PROSECUTING
ATTORNEY: You were never required
                        to investigate
                        the reasons for the hangings and shootings

ACCUSED #1: It wasn't my job
                        to concern myself with them

PROSECUTING
ATTORNEY: As adjutant to the camp commander
                        what were your duties then

ACCUSED #1: I calculated operating costs
                        charted the distribution of the labor supply
                        and processed personnel files
                        I was also required to accompany
                        the commanding officer to receptions
                        and command the honor guard

PROSECUTING
ATTORNEY: When was the honor guard used

ACCUSED #1: On ceremonial occasions
                        and for burials
                        A funeral procession
                        was trooped for the burials

PROSECUTING
ATTORNEY: Whose burial

ACCUSED #1: The burial of an officer
PROSECUTING
ATTORNEY: Who was notified
                        of deaths among the prisoners

ACCUSED #1: I don't know
                        Perhaps the Political Division

PROSECUTING
ATTORNEY: Weren't you informed
                   that from 100 to 200 prisoners
                   died daily in the camp

ACCUSED #1:   I don't recall
                   ever having seen
                   comparative daily reports
                   of the camp population
                   On any given day
                   10 or 15 discharges might be reported
                   but numbers in the amount
                   mentioned here
                   I never heard

PROSECUTING
ATTORNEY: You didn't know about the mass killings
                   in the gas chambers

ACCUSED #1:   I didn't know anything about them

PROSECUTING
ATTORNEY: You never noticed the smoke
                   from the chimneys of the crematoriums
                   smoke that was visible for miles

ACCUSED #1:   After all it was a big camp
                   with its natural rate of discharge
                   and they had to be burned

PROSECUTING
ATTORNEY: You never noticed
                   the condition of the prisoners

ACCUSED #1:   It was a penal camp
                   People weren't there for their health

PROSECUTING
ATTORNEY: As adjutant to the camp's commanding officer

weren't you interested in
how the prisoners were fed and quartered

ACCUSED #1: I never heard of any complaints

PROSECUTING
ATTORNEY: Didn't you ever discuss
occurrences in the camp
with your commanding officer

ACCUSED #1: No
There were no exceptional occurrences

PROSECUTING
ATTORNEY: From your point of view
what was the purpose of the camp

ACCUSED #1: The purpose of a protective-custody camp
was to educate enemies of the state
to a different way of thinking
It was not my job
to question this purpose

PROSECUTING
ATTORNEY: Did you know
the significance of the designation
special treatment

ACCUSED #1: That was a government secret
of the highest priority
I couldn't know anything about it
Anyone who spoke of it
risked the death penalty

PROSECUTING
ATTORNEY: Nevertheless you did know about it

ACCUSED #1: I cannot answer that

PROSECUTING
ATTORNEY: What did you do for the troops

ACCUSED #1:   There was a theater and a movie house
                and entertainment evenings
                Mr Knittel took care of that
                and also held evening classes
                for the officers

PROSECUTING
ATTORNEY: Was he trained to do that

ACCUSED #1:   He was a high-school teacher
                and if I am correctly informed
                he is presently a principal
                at a school somewhere
                a man obviously suited
                for the teaching profession

PROSECUTING
ATTORNEY: And you instructed
                the troops in ideological matters

COUNSEL FOR
THE DEFENSE: We advise our client
                that he need not reply
                to questions put to him
                by the assistant prosecuting attorney

PROSECUTING
ATTORNEY: The decision on this matter
                rests solely
                with the accused
                By intervening at this point
                the defense grossly exceeds
                its legitimate authority
                It is obvious
                that by resorting to such tactics
                the defense is attempting to prevent us
                from determining the truth

COUNSEL FOR
THE DEFENSE: In reply to this astonishing performance
                we must vigorously protest

At this point it becomes quite clear
that the prosecution
is not familiar with the rules obtaining in
these present proceedings
that they simply don't know the law
The prosecution
initiated these proceedings
already prejudiced
>   [*The Accused laugh nodding in agree-
>   ment*]

THE SONG OF THE POSSIBILITY
OF SURVIVAL

II

3RD WITNESS: The power
of any member of the camp personnel
was unlimited
They were free
each one of them
to kill
or to save
I saw Dr Flage standing by a fence
with tears in his eyes
looking at a trainload of children
being taken to the crematorium
He did nothing to stop me
from holding on to the files
of patients already selected
and thus preventing their death
Camp Doctor Flage showed me
it was possible
to see the one living person
among the thousands
He showed me
that it would have been possible
to influence the course of the camp operation
if there had been others
like him

COUNSEL FOR
THE DEFENSE: As a prisoner doctor
did you have the power to determine
whether your patient
should live or die

3RD WITNESS: I could occasionally
save a life

COUNSEL FOR
THE DEFENSE: Yet weren't you also required
to select patients to be killed

3RD WITNESS: There was nothing I could do
about changing the required quota
That was set by the camp administration
Still it was possible
to alter the lists

COUNSEL FOR
THE DEFENSE: When it came to choosing
between one patient and another
what determined your choice

3RD WITNESS: We had to weigh
which of the two was more likely
to survive his illness
Then there was the far
more difficult question
which of the two would be useful
to the internal affairs of the prisoners

COUNSEL FOR
THE DEFENSE: Were some especially preferred

3RD WITNESS: Politically active prisoners
naturally stuck together
supported and helped each other
as much as they could
Since I belonged to the resistance movement
within the camp
I of course did all I could
to keep others in the movement alive

COUNSEL FOR
THE DEFENSE: What could the resistance movement
accomplish in the camp

3RD WITNESS: The chief aim of the resistance
was to keep alive our sense of solidarity
Furthermore we documented
everything that went on in the camp
and buried our evidence
in tin cans

COUNSEL FOR
THE DEFENSE: Did you have any contact with partisans
or any connection with the outside world

3RD WITNESS: Prisoners assigned to factory work
could occasionally establish contact
with partisans
and they were able to give us reports
about the situation at the various fronts

COUNSEL FOR
THE DEFENSE: Were preparations made
for an armed rising in the camp

3RD WITNESS: We managed to
smuggle in dynamite later on

COUNSEL FOR
THE DEFENSE: Was the camp ever attacked
from the outside or by any groups inside

3RD WITNESS: In the last winter of the war
the special commandos
that worked in the crematoriums
revolted
The revolt was unsuccessful
That was the only active attempt
From the outside
no attempt was made

COUNSEL FOR
THE DEFENSE: Did you ever request aid
through your contacts

3RD WITNESS: Reports on conditions in the camp
were smuggled out time and again

COUNSEL FOR
THE DEFENSE: What did you hope would come
of getting these reports out

3RD WITNESS: We hoped for an air raid
on the gas chambers
or that the railroad tracks
leading
into the camp
would be bombed

COUNSEL FOR
THE DEFENSE: When you saw
that you were left quite alone
every form of military assistance denied you
how were you able to sustain
your will to resist

3RD WITNESS: Considering our situation
it was resistance enough
just to keep alert
and never give up the thought
that someday there would come a time
when we could speak out
and tell what we had seen
and lived through

COUNSEL FOR
THE DEFENSE: How did you
justify what you had to do
with the oath you had taken as a doctor

PROSECUTING
ATTORNEY: We object to this question
which the defense has raised
solely to blur the distinction between
witness and accused

The accused killed of their own free choice
The witness was forced
to be present at the killings

3RD WITNESS: I would like to reply to the question
Those prisoners who
by their privileged position in the camp
managed to postpone their own death
had at least to some degree
defied their masters
In order to maintain the possibility of survival
they were forced
to give the appearance of cooperating
I saw that demonstrated very clearly
in the infirmary
I soon became bound to the staff doctors
not only because of our professional relationship
but also through my complicity
in the workings of the camp system
Every prisoner
from those who held the most privileged posi-
tions
down to those who were dying
was part of that system
The difference
between us and the camp personnel
was less than what separated us
from those who were outside

COUNSEL FOR
THE DEFENSE: Do you mean to say
there was an understanding
between the administration and the prisoner

3RD WITNESS: When we talk of our experience nowadays
with people who never were in a camp

there is always something
inconceivable to them about it
And yet they are the same people
who in the camp were prisoners and guards
Since such a great number of us
came into the camp
and since the number of those
who brought us there was also great
one would think that what happened then
would still be comprehensible today
Many of those who were destined
to play the part of prisoners
had grown up with the same ideas
the same way of looking at things
as those
who found themselves acting as guards
They were all equally dedicated
to the same nation
to its prosperity
and its rewards
And if they had not been designated
prisoners
they could equally well have been guards
We must drop the lofty view
that the camp world
is incomprehensible to us
We all knew the society
that produced a government
capable of creating such camps
The order that prevailed there
was an order whose basic nature
we were familiar with
For that very reason
we were able to find our way about
in its logical and ultimate consequence
where the oppressor

could expand his authority
to a degree never known before
and the oppressed
was forced to yield up
the fertilizing dust
of his bones

COUNSEL FOR
THE DEFENSE: We utterly reject
theories of this kind
theories that reflect
a completely distorted
ideological point of view

3RD WITNESS: It is true
most of the prisoners
spilling out of the freight cars
onto the platform
had no time to comprehend
what was happening to them
Baffled and speechless
they walked that final path
and let themselves be killed
because they understood nothing
We call them heroes
but their death was pointless
We can see them before us
these millions
lit by searchlights
standing in a din of curses
and barking dogs
Today the outside world wonders
how they could have
let themselves be destroyed that way
We
who still live with these pictures
know that millions could stand again

waiting to be destroyed
and that the new destruction
will be far more efficient
than the old one was

COUNSEL FOR
THE DEFENSE: Was the witness
politically active
even before being sent
to the camp

3RD WITNESS: Yes
It was our strength
that we knew
why we were there
It helped us
preserve our identity
But even that strength
sustained only a handful
to the moment of their death
They could be broken too

7TH WITNESS: There were 1200 of us
who were led off to the crematoriums
We had to wait a long time
since there was another shipment
ahead of us
I was standing a little to one side
A prisoner walked by
He was very young
He whispered
Get away from here
I picked up my shoes and walked off
I went around a corner
There was another prisoner there
Where are you going
he asked

They sent me away
I answered
Then come with me
he said
So I got back into the camp

COUNSEL FOR
THE DEFENSE: Was it that simple
You could just walk away

7TH WITNESS: I don't know how it was with others
I walked off
and went into the infirmary
The prisoner doctor asked me
Do you want to live
I said yes
He looked at me for a while
then he found a place for me there

COUNSEL FOR
THE DEFENSE: And so you survived
your stay in the camp

7TH WITNESS: I came out of the camp
yes
but the camp is still there

THE SONG OF THE POSSIBILITY
OF SURVIVAL

III

JUDGE: The witness
spent several months
in women's Barrack Number 10
Medical experiments
were made there
What can you tell us about them

4TH WITNESS: [*Remains silent*]

JUDGE: The court can well understand
that you must find it difficult to speak
and that you prefer to remain silent
Yet we request you
to search your memory
for anything that may
shed light on the events
under consideration here today

4TH WITNESS: There were about 600 of us there
Professor Clauberg directed the research
The rest of the camp doctors supplied him
with the subjects he worked on

JUDGE: Could you describe the experiments

4TH WITNESS: [*Remains silent*]
COUNSEL FOR
THE DEFENSE: Does the witness
suffer from lapses of memory

4TH WITNESS: I have been ill
since my time in the camp

COUNSEL FOR
THE DEFENSE: What are the symptoms of your illness

4TH WITNESS: Dizzy spells and nausea
Earlier I had to throw up in the bathroom
because it smelled of chlorine
Chlorine was poured over the corpses
I can't stand to be in locked rooms

COUNSEL FOR
THE DEFENSE: No loss of memory

4TH WITNESS: I would like to forget
but I keep seeing it
I would like to have the number on my arm
removed
In the summer
when I wear sleeveless dresses
people stare at it
and I always see the same look
in their eyes

COUNSEL FOR
THE DEFENSE: What look

4TH WITNESS: Scorn

JUDGE: Does the witness
feel she is still being persecuted

4TH WITNESS: [*Remains silent*]

JUDGE: What experiments
does the witness recall

4TH WITNESS: There were girls there

                    17 or 18 years old
                    They were chosen
                    from the healthiest prisoners
                    They were used for X-ray experiments

JUDGE: Could you describe these experiments

4TH WITNESS: The girls were placed
                    in front of the X-ray machines
                    A metal plate was attached
                    to their stomachs and buttocks
                    The X-rays were directed at their ovaries
                    which were burned out
                    Burns and running sores developed
                    on their stomachs and buttocks as a result

JUDGE: What was done with these girls

4TH WITNESS: Within the next three months
                    they were operated on
                    a number of times

JUDGE: What kind of operations were these

4TH WITNESS: Their ovaries and gonads
                    were removed

JUDGE: Did the patients die

4TH WITNESS: If they didn't die during the experiment
                    they died soon after
                    After a few weeks the girls
                    had changed completely
                    They looked like old women

JUDGE: Could you

tell us if any of the accused present
took part in these experiments

4TH WITNESS: All the doctors came together daily
in their quarters
It would seem likely that at the least
they knew what was going on

COUNSEL FOR
THE DEFENSE: We strenuously object
to loose allegations of this kind
The mere fact that our clients
were in the vicinity when these events occurred
by no means
implicates them as accessories

JUDGE: Would the witness
tell us what other experiments were under-
taken

4TH WITNESS: [*Remains silent*]
COUNSEL FOR
THE DEFENSE: It is our opinion
that because of the witness' obvious ill-health
she is incapable
of providing the court with credible evidence

PROSECUTING
ATTORNEY: Could you
describe for the court other experiments
which you witnessed yourself

4TH WITNESS: A syringe
with a tube attachment
was used to inject a fluid
into the womb

JUDGE: What kind of fluid was it

4TH WITNESS: It was a cement paste
that burned and hurt like labor pains
The women could only walk stooped
to the X-ray table
where a picture was taken

JUDGE: What was the purpose of the injection

4TH WITNESS: The fallopian tubes would be glued together
to prevent conception

JUDGE: Were the same patients
subjected to repeated experiments

4TH WITNESS: After the injection of the paste
a contract fluid
was injected for X-ray observation
Then the paste
was pumped in once again
This process
might be repeated many times
at three- to four-week intervals
Infection of the womb
or of the stomach lining
caused most the deaths
I never saw anyone sterilize
medical instruments
between treatments

JUDGE: How many such experiments would you estimate
were carried out

4TH WITNESS: During the six months
I spent in Barrack Number 10
400

            In connection with these experiments
            there were others
            in artificial insemination
            If a woman got pregnant
            an abortion was induced

JUDGE: In what month of the pregnancy was that
            done

4TH WITNESS: In the seventh month
            A variety of X-ray experiments were made
            throughout the pregnancy
            After the abortion
            if by any chance the child was still alive
            it was killed and dissected

COUNSEL FOR
THE DEFENSE: Are the witness' statements
            based on hearsay
            or on firsthand knowledge

4TH WITNESS: I speak from personal experience
COUNSEL FOR
THE DEFENSE: What saved you then

4TH WITNESS: The evacuation of the camp

THE SONG OF
THE DEATH OF LILI TOFLER

I

JUDGE: Is the name of Lili Tofler
familiar to the witness

5TH WITNESS: Yes
It is
Lili Tofler was an unusually
pretty girl
She was arrested
because she wrote a letter
to a prisoner
When she tried
to smuggle it in to the prisoner
the letter was found
Lili Tofler was interrogated
They wanted the prisoner's name
Boger was in charge of the interrogation
At his order
Lili Tofler was taken to the prison bunker
There she was stood up naked
against the wall
They went through the whole procedure
time and again
exactly as if she was going to be shot
All the orders were called out
but they didn't shoot
Finally she got down on her knees
and begged them to shoot her

JUDGE: Was she shot

5TH WITNESS: Yes

6TH WITNESS: I was under bunker arrest
when Lili Tofler was brought in
with two other prisoners
who had been involved
in the smuggling of the letter
Once during that time
Jakob
the special-duty prisoner
in charge of the bunker
let me use the washroom
I saw the girl lying dead on the floor
Boger killed the other prisoners later
out in the courtyard

JUDGE: Accused Boger
are you familiar with this case

ACCUSED #2: That Lili Tofler was executed
is true
As a typist in the Political Division
she had access to confidential files
and was forbidden all contact
with other prisoners
I had nothing to do
with her being killed
I was as shaken to hear of her death
as the Bunker-Jakob
whose face was covered with tears

JUDGE: Can you tell us
what was in the letter

ACCUSED #2: No

JUDGE:	Does the witness know what was in the letter
5TH WITNESS:	In the letter Lili Tofler asked if they would ever be able to go on living after the things they had seen and experienced there I remember too that she went on to ask her friend if he had gotten her previous letter She also wrote about some encouraging news she had heard
COUNSEL FOR THE DEFENSE:	How did you come to know this
5TH WITNESS:	Lili Tofler was a friend of mine We lived in the same barrack She talked to me about the letter Later I saw the letter I worked in the Camp Registry Office Lili Tofler's death certificate was sent there The letter was attached
JUDGE:	Did you know the prisoner to whom the letter was addressed
5TH WITNESS:	Yes
JUDGE:	Did Lili Tofler betray his name
5TH WITNESS:	No The prisoners had to line up on the assembly ground Lili was supposed to pick him out

I remember exactly
even now
how she stood in front of him
looked into his eyes
and then went on
without saying a word

COUNSEL FOR
THE DEFENSE: Were you required to appear
for the line-up too

5TH WITNESS: Yes
COUNSEL FOR
THE DEFENSE: Where was the assembly ground

5TH WITNESS: It was the street and the open space
in front of the kitchen barracks
in the old camp
COUNSEL FOR
THE DEFENSE: Would you describe the assembly ground

5TH WITNESS: To the right of the gallows
was the small guardhouse
where officers stood
to take the roll call
Its walls were wood
painted to look like stone
On top of the pitched roof
was a weathervane
It looked like a toy house
There were poplars on both sides of the street
The prisoners stood in the street
and in between the barracks
Lili Tofler was led along in front of them
It was on that same day
that I saw
what was painted on the kitchen roof

It was painted in large letters
THERE IS ONE WAY TO FREEDOM
ITS MILESTONES ARE
OBEDIENCE DILIGENCE CLEANLINESS
HONESTY TRUTHFULNESS
AND LOVE OF COUNTRY

JUDGE: Was the prisoner
                to whom the letter was addressed
                ever discovered

5TH WITNESS: No

THE SONG OF
THE DEATH OF LILI TOFLER

II

JUDGE: You were in charge
of the agricultural operations of the camp
At the time of her arrest
Lili Tofler was working
in one of the offices
under your supervision
What did she do there

1ST WITNESS: She did drafting
or typing
I can't remember which

JUDGE: Had she been transferred to you
from the Political Division

1ST WITNESS: It's been so long now I couldn't say
Our operation had no direct connection
with the camp
We were under the jurisdiction
of the S.S. Office of Economy
Since we were growing rubber plants
our operations were essential
to the war effort
Basically my duties
were of a purely scientific nature

JUDGE: Do you recall
the arrest
of Lili Tofler

1ST WITNESS: As I remember
it had something to do with a letter

JUDGE: Do you know
that Lili Tofler was arrested
because of this letter

1ST WITNESS: I believe
the letter was found in a shipment of carrots

JUDGE: What was the shipment for

1ST WITNESS: They were carrots we grew
for the medical section

JUDGE: For what purpose

1ST WITNESS: I assume
they were used for special diets
Professor Clauberg had ordered them

JUDGE: What did you know
about Professor Clauberg's work

1ST WITNESS: They carried out research there
commissioned by various
pharmaceutical concerns

JUDGE: What kind of research

1ST WITNESS: That I don't know
All I knew about the camp
was that it had to do with
a large industrial complex
and that its various branches
employed prisoners as labor supply

PROSECUTING
ATTORNEY: To which of these branches
               did your operation belong

1ST WITNESS: We were a subdivision of the Buna Works
               of I-G Farben
               We were engaged in war production
PROSECUTING
ATTORNEY: Were you aware
               that prisoners had been projected
               as the labor supply
               when these industries were established

1ST WITNESS: Yes
               naturally
PROSECUTING
ATTORNEY: Did the industries
               pay wages for prisoner labor

1ST WITNESS: Of course they did
               There were established rates
PROSECUTING
ATTORNEY: What were the rates

1ST WITNESS: For a skilled worker a dollar a day
               For an unskilled 75 cents
PROSECUTING
ATTORNEY: How long was the work day

1ST WITNESS: 11 hours
PROSECUTING
ATTORNEY: To whom were the wages paid

1ST WITNESS: To the camp administration
               After all
               they had to provide for the prisoners

PROSECUTING
ATTORNEY: Didn't you know
that the prisoners were
used up and then killed

1ST WITNESS: I always tried to help the prisoners
more so in fact than I had any right to
I suffered
when I saw
how the prisoners assigned to my operation
had to walk all those miles every day
from their barracks over to the work camp
I made use
of every available emergency measure
to ensure that our prisoners
got better care
and a good pair of shoes

PROSECUTING
ATTORNEY: How many prisoners were employed
in your operation

1ST WITNESS: 5 to 6 hundred

PROSECUTING
ATTORNEY: Didn't you ever notice
the frequent turnover
in the make-up of the work details

1ST WITNESS: I did what I could
to hold on to my people

PROSECUTING
ATTORNEY: Did any of them get sick

1ST WITNESS: Naturally
I knew of course about the epidemics
that afflicted the prisoners in the camp

PROSECUTING
ATTORNEY: You didn't notice

that prisoners on the sick list
never returned

1ST WITNESS: No
Frequently they did come back
from the infirmary

PROSECUTING
ATTORNEY: Did you hear of any mistreatment in the camp

1ST WITNESS: Heard about it
yes

PROSECUTING
ATTORNEY: What did you hear

1ST WITNESS: I heard
they were beaten

PROSECUTING
ATTORNEY: Who beat them

1ST WITNESS: I don't know
I never saw it happen
I just heard about it

PROSECUTING
ATTORNEY: Did you know about
the extermination program

1ST WITNESS: If you were there three years
naturally something leaked out
You knew what was going on
but later on
when I heard the numbers involved
I simply couldn't grasp it

PROSECUTING
ATTORNEY: You never saw any of the transports

1ST WITNESS: A couple of times at the most

PROSECUTING
ATTORNEY: Do you know any of the accused present here

1ST WITNESS: I know some of them
Mainly the group leaders
We used to meet
in their club
on a purely social basis

PROSECUTING
ATTORNEY: Today you hold a high
advisory position in the government
Did you meet these men again
after the war
when most of them
had returned to civilian life

1ST WITNESS: I may have met one or another of them

PROSECUTING
ATTORNEY: On such occasions
did you ever talk about
the events of those days

1ST WITNESS: Mr Prosecutor
we were all concerned with
one thing
winning the war

PROSECUTING
ATTORNEY: The court has summoned as witnesses
three former directors
of factories attached to the camp
One of these witnesses
has submitted to the court a sworn affidavit
stating that he is blind
and therefore cannot appear
The second suffers from a fractured spine
Only one former chairman of the board
has come

Would the witness
tell us if he is still connected
with the firms
which formerly employed prisoners

COUNSEL FOR
THE DEFENSE: We object to this question
which has no other motive
than to undermine public confidence
in our industrial concerns

2ND WITNESS: I am no longer actively engaged
in business

PROSECUTING
ATTORNEY: Do you receive a pension
from these concerns

2ND WITNESS: Yes

PROSECUTING
ATTORNEY: Does this pension amount to
75,000 dollars a year

COUNSEL FOR
THE DEFENSE: We object to the question

PROSECUTING
ATTORNEY: Now that you live in your castle
and are no longer engaged
with the business of your concern
which has only changed by changing its name
what do you do

2ND WITNESS: I collect porcelain
paintings and engravings
as well as various objects of folk art

COUNSEL FOR
THE DEFENSE: Questions of this nature
are entirely irrelevant
to the stated purpose of these proceedings

PROSECUTING
ATTORNEY: As a representative of the camp industries
               you were directly responsible
               for assigning prisoners to the factories
               What can you tell us about the agreement
               arrived at between these industries
               and the camp administration
               relating to prisoners
               no longer fit for work

2ND WITNESS: I know nothing about that
PROSECUTING
ATTORNEY: The court has in its possession
               weekly reports which deal with prisoners found
               by the management of these industries
               to be too weak to do their work

2ND WITNESS: I don't know anything about that
PROSECUTING
ATTORNEY: Didn't you ever notice the physical condition
               of the prisoners

2ND WITNESS: I personally did everything
               I could to prevent the utilization
               of a labor force
               composed of asocial
               or politically unreliable elements

PROSECUTING
ATTORNEY: The court has in its record
               a letter which mentions
               the happy and prosperous friendship
               existing between your firm
               and the camp administration
               Among other things
               the letter goes on to say
               At dinner
               we made further use of the occasion

to draw up measures
advantageous to the Buna Works
that relate to the merger
of the truly outstanding
operations of the camp
What were those measures

2ND WITNESS: I simply had to do my duty
and to see to it
that government requisitions
were met

PROSECUTING
ATTORNEY: Will you not
speak out clearly
to corroborate
what a previous witness pointed out
the system of exploitation
that existed in the camp
By the limitless grinding down of people
you
as well as the other directors
of the large firms involved
made profits
that annually amounted to billions

COUNSEL FOR
THE DEFENSE: Objection

PROSECUTING
ATTORNEY: Let us once more bring to mind
that the successors to those same concerns
have ended up today in magnificent condition
and that they are now in the midst of
as they say
a new phase of expansion

COUNSEL FOR
THE DEFENSE: We call upon the court
to make a record
of this slander

THE SONG OF
THE DEATH OF LILI TOFLER

III

JUDGE: What do you know of the arrest
                    of Lili Tofler

1ST WITNESS: I don't know what happened
                    All I remember is
                    that she was taken away
                    I asked what was going on and heard
                    they were still investigating the matter
                    Later I heard
                    they had killed her

JUDGE: Who killed her

1ST WITNESS: I don't know
                    I wasn't there

JUDGE: You were at that time a brigadier general
                    which meant you ranked
                    between a colonel and a major general
                    Was there no way you could have intervened
                    when one of your workers was taken away

1ST WITNESS: I wasn't
                    sufficiently informed about the case

JUDGE: You made no inquiries
                    about the cause of her arrest

1ST WITNESS: That was beyond my jurisdiction

JUDGE: Yet that constituted a gross interference
in your personal sphere of activity
A person whom you needed
for work essential to the war effort
was simply removed from your laboratory

1ST WITNESS: Lili Tofler was not an outstanding worker

JUDGE: But you greatly outranked
any man in the Political Division
Why did you tolerate this invasion
of your own area of responsibility

1ST WITNESS: Mr Chairman
there was an unwritten law then
that applied to everybody
It was
Take care about doing favors for prisoners
You could go just so far
but no further

JUDGE: The court calls as witness
the prisoner
to whom Lili Tofler
wrote the previously mentioned letter
Would you tell us
how you managed to survive

9TH WITNESS: A few days after she had been
taken to the bunker
I was brought there too
I thought
Lili had betrayed me

but I was just one of many
that had been brought in as hostages
I heard there
that every morning and every afternoon
Lili had to stand in the washroom for an hour
The whole time she was in there Boger kept
a pistol pressed against her head
That went on for four days
Then I was taken out
with a group of 50 prisoners
to be shot
All that time I thought
Boger must know
the letter was meant for me
I saw the clerk put a cross
next to my name on the list
On paper I was already dead
The prisoners were taken out to the yard
and shot
Only two
for some reason
were left behind
I was one of them
I was still in the hallway
when suddenly the Bunker-Jakob came
and pulled me back out into the yard
I thought
Now I'm going to be shot
But he just showed me the pile
of dead comrades
On top lay the two prisoners
who had smuggled the letter into the camp
Over to one side was Lili
with two holes in her heart
I asked Jakob
who had shot her

He said
Boger

JUDGE: Accused Boger
do you have anything to add

ACCUSED #2: No
thank you

JUDGE: Where did Lili Tofler originally come from

5TH WITNESS: I don't know where she came from

JUDGE: What was she like

5TH WITNESS: Whenever I met Lili
and asked her
How are you Lili
she said
Fine
I am always fine

THE SONG OF S.S. CORPORAL STARK

I

8TH WITNESS: The accused Stark
was in charge of the Reception Squad
I was assigned to the squad as a clerk
Stark was 20 years old then
In his free time
he used to study for his high-school finals
To test himself on the subjects
Stark enjoyed putting all sorts of questions
to the college graduates among the prisoners
On the evening
the Polish woman with the two children
was brought in
he was discussing
aspects of humanism in Goethe with us

JUDGE: What was the reason
for their being brought in

8TH WITNESS: We only found that out later
The eight-year-old boy
had picked up a rabbit and given it
to the woman's two-year-old daughter
to play with
The rabbit belonged to a camp official
So all three
were to be shot
Stark
carried out the execution

JUDGE: Could you see the execution

8TH WITNESS: Executions were carried out
in the old crematorium in those days
The crematorium was directly
behind the reception barrack
Through the window
we could see Stark
with the woman and two children
go into the crematorium
He had his rifle slung over his shoulder
We heard a series of shots
Then Stark came out alone

JUDGE: Accused Stark
does this description correspond to the facts

ACCUSED #12: I completely reject it

JUDGE: What was your rank in the camp

ACCUSED #12: I was barrack-leader

JUDGE: How did you come there

ACCUSED #12: I was assigned to camp duty
along with a group
of other noncommissioned officers

JUDGE: Were you made barrack-leader
right from the start

ACCUSED #12: That's what we were meant for
that's what we were used for

JUDGE: Were you trained
for this assignment

ACCUSED #12: We had our leadership course behind us

JUDGE: Were you given any general instructions
for your task in the camp

ACCUSED #12: Only a short indoctrination period

JUDGE: What happened when you arrived at the camp

ACCUSED #12: There was a reception commission

JUDGE: Made up of whom

ACCUSED #12: The commanding officer and the adjutant
the protective-custody camp leader
and the chief clerk

JUDGE: What assignment were you given

ACCUSED #12: I was first assigned to a prisoner barrack
Most of them were young
High-school and university students

JUDGE: Why were they in the camp

ACCUSED #12: I believe
it was because of their contact
with the resistance movement
It was a collective sentence
They had been transferred there
by Security Police Command Headquarters

JUDGE: Did you see their admission orders

ACCUSED #12: No
It wasn't any of my business either

JUDGE: What did you have to do then

ACCUSED #12: I had to see to it
that the people got to work on time
and that the numbers checked out

JUDGE: Were there any attempts to escape

ACCUSED #12: Not under my command

JUDGE: Were the people adequately provided for

ACCUSED #12: They each got their quart of soup

JUDGE: What happened
if the people could not
or would not work

ACCUSED #12: That didn't happen

JUDGE: Didn't you ever have cause to take action
when prisoners broke rules

ACCUSED #12: That never came up
I never had to turn in a report

JUDGE: You never struck anyone

ACCUSED #12: I never had to

JUDGE: When were you transferred
to the Reception Section
of the Political Division

ACCUSED #12: May 1941

JUDGE: What was the reason
for your being transferred

ACCUSED #12:I used to go riding
One of the men I got to know that way
was the chief of the Political Division
Lieutenant Grabner
He asked me what I was by profession
When I told him I was a student
studying for my final exams
he said
they were looking for people like me
A few days later
I received my transfer orders

JUDGE: What were your duties
in the Reception Section

ACCUSED #12:The first thing I had to do
was to familiarize myself
with the registration
Incoming prisoners were
provided with a number
After that
personnel records had to be set up
and index cards filled out

JUDGE: How did the prisoners arrive

ACCUSED #12:They were marched in
trucked in
or they came by train
Trains arrived every Tuesday
Thursday and Friday

JUDGE: What was the reception procedure

ACCUSED #12:I had to stand by
when transports were announced

First
prisoners were assembled
in front of the camp entrance
then the transport leader
handed over the transport papers
to Reception
Prisoners fell in for the count
and were issued their numbers
At that time
numbers were not yet tattooed
Each prisoner was issued a number
in triplicate on cardboard
One number he kept
one went with personal effects
one was attached to valuables
He had to retain his cardboard number
until he was issued a cloth one

JUDGE: What was your part in this procedure

ACCUSED #12: I handed out the numbers
and conducted the prisoners
to the personal-effects barrack
There prisoners were stripped
showered and dressed
Their hair was cut
Then they were received
by Reception

JUDGE: What did that entail

ACCUSED #12: Personnel records were filled out
Questionnaires made up for Reception
were taken to the Reception office
An admissions list was then drawn up
listing the different categories

                    political prisoners
                    criminal prisoners
                    and racial prisoners
                    This list was then circulated
                    to the various sections

JUDGE: To which sections

ACCUSED #12: To the protective-custody camp leader
                    to headquarters
                    to the Political Division
                    and to the doctors
                    12 copies went out for distribution
                    with the daily dispatches

JUDGE: Did you have anything more to do
                    with the prisoners

ACCUSED #12: After Reception
                    for me they were over and done with

PROSECUTING
ATTORNEY: Accused Stark
                    were you on hand
                    for the arrival of all transports

ACCUSED #12: It was my duty to be present
PROSECUTING
ATTORNEY: When transports arrived
                    what were your duties

ACCUSED #12: All I had to do there
                    was manage the record traffic
PROSECUTING
ATTORNEY: What does that mean

ACCUSED #12: Some of the prisoners were held over
                    These I had to enter in the book

PROSECUTING
ATTORNEY: And the others

ACCUSED #12:The others were transferred
PROSECUTING
ATTORNEY: What was the difference

ACCUSED #12:Prisoners held over
                went to the camp
                Transferred prisoners
                were neither received
                nor admitted
                That is the difference
                between held over
                and transferred
PROSECUTING
ATTORNEY: What happened to the transferred prisoners

ACCUSED #12:They were taken directly
                to the small crematorium
                for extermination
PROSECUTING
ATTORNEY: Was this before the construction
                of the big crematoriums

ACCUSED #12:The big crematoriums in the outer camp
                first went into operation
                in the summer of 1942
                Until then the crematorium
                in the old camp was used
PROSECUTING
ATTORNEY: How were the prisoners transferred

ACCUSED #12:Lists were compared
                and names crossed out

                    Prisoners who were not
                    to be received into the camp
                    were marched into the small crematorium

PROSECUTING
ATTORNEY: What were they told

ACCUSED #12: They were informed
                    that they were going to be disinfected

PROSECUTING
ATTORNEY: Weren't they uneasy

ACCUSED #12: No
                    They went in quietly

THE SONG OF S.S. CORPORAL STARK

II

8TH WITNESS: We knew exactly how Stark would behave
when he came back from a killing
Everything in the room
had to be in order and absolutely clean
and we had to chase the flies out
with handkerchiefs
If he spotted a fly
he would go into a rage
Even before he took off his cap
he would wash his hands in a basin
his flunkey always had ready for him
on a stool next to the door
When he had washed his hands
he pointed at the dirty water
and the flunkey had to run out
for more
Then he handed us his jacket to be cleaned
and washed his hands and face again

7TH WITNESS: I see Stark always
all the time
I can hear him call
Move
get in
move you pigs
And then we had to go into the chamber

JUDGE: What chamber

7TH WITNESS: The chamber in the old crematorium

Several hundred
women and children
lay there like packages
There were prisoners of war in there too
Move
Get their clothes off
Stark yelled
I was 18 years old
and I had never seen a corpse before
I just stood there
Then Stark started beating me

JUDGE: Were there wounds on the dead

7TH WITNESS: Yes

JUDGE: Were they bullet wounds

7TH WITNESS: No
                They had been gassed
                They were heaped up stiff
                on top of each other
                Sometimes when we pulled
                their clothes ripped
                Then we were beaten again

JUDGE: Weren't the people required
                to undress first

7TH WITNESS: That was later
                in the new crematoriums
                where there were rooms for that

JUDGE: Was Stark present there too

7TH WITNESS: Stark was always present

I can hear him shouting
Move
Get those rags
Once a small man hid himself
under a pile of clothes
Stark found him
Come here he shouted
and pushed him up against the wall
He shot him first in one leg
and then in the other
Finally he slid down on a bench
and then Stark shot him dead
He always liked to shoot the legs first
Once I heard a woman scream
Captain
I didn't do anything
He yelled
Get up against the wall Sarah
The woman begged him not to kill her
Then he started shooting

JUDGE: When did you
first see the accused Stark
at these killings

7TH WITNESS: In the fall of 1941

JUDGE: Were these the first killings
by gas

7TH WITNESS: Yes

JUDGE: Would you describe the old crematorium

7TH WITNESS: It was built of concrete
It had a thick square chimney

The walls were covered by
sloping embankments
The chamber was about 20 yards long
and five yards wide
You had to pass through a small anteroom
first
On the other side of the chamber
a door led to the first oven
and a second door to a room
with the two other ovens

JUDGE: Accused Stark
             how large were the groups
             you had to conduct to the crematoriums

ACCUSED #12: On the average
             150 to 200 head

JUDGE: Were women and children among them

ACCUSED #12: Yes

JUDGE: Did you think it right
             that women and children
             should be a part of these transports

ACCUSED #12: Yes
             The Family Liability Laws
             were in effect then

JUDGE: You did not question
             the guilt of these women and children

ACCUSED #12: We had been told
             they had actively participated
             in poisoning springs and wells

                        blowing up bridges
                        and other acts of sabotage

JUDGE: Did you also see prisoners of war
                        among these people

ACCUSED #12:Yes
                        Those prisoners had
                        by issued order
                        lost all claim to decent treatment

PROSECUTING
ATTORNEY: Accused Stark
                        in the fall of 1941
                        a large number of Soviet
                        prisoners of war
                        were brought to the camp
                        According to court records
                        you were instrumental
                        in processing these contingents

ACCUSED #12:In connection with these transports
                        I only followed instructions

PROSECUTING
ATTORNEY: What did that mean

ACCUSED #12:I simply had to march them off
                        take over their cards marked
                        for execution
                        destroy their identification tags
                        and enter their numbers in the file

PROSECUTING
ATTORNEY: What reason
                        was given for the execution
                        of these prisoners of war

ACCUSED #12:We were dealing with the annihilation

of an ideology
With their fanatical political orientation
these prisoners constituted a threat
to camp security

PROSECUTING
ATTORNEY: Where were the executions carried out

ACCUSED #12:In the courtyard of Barrack 11
PROSECUTING
ATTORNEY: Did you take part in the executions

ACCUSED #12:In one instance
               yes
PROSECUTING
ATTORNEY: What was the procedure

ACCUSED #12:The roll was called
               and the formalities concluded
               They were taken out to the courtyard
               one after the other
               It was almost over
               Then Grabner said
               Stark you carry on
               Up to then the other corporals
               had been taking turns

PROSECUTING
ATTORNEY: How many did you shoot

ACCUSED #12:I can't remember
PROSECUTING
ATTORNEY: More than one

ACCUSED #12:Yes
PROSECUTING
ATTORNEY: More than two

ACCUSED #12: Four or five possibly

PROSECUTING
ATTORNEY: Did you try
               to get out of taking part in the execution

ACCUSED #12: But it was an order
               It was my duty as a soldier

PROSECUTING
ATTORNEY: Did you participate
               in any other executions

ACCUSED #12: No
               I was given leave
               to complete my studies

PROSECUTING
ATTORNEY: When did your leave begin

ACCUSED #12: In December 1941

PROSECUTING
ATTORNEY: When did you complete your studies

ACCUSED #12: I passed my examinations
               in the spring of 1942

PROSECUTING
ATTORNEY: Did you then
               return to the camp

ACCUSED #12: For a short time yes

COUNSEL FOR
THE DEFENSE: We would like to call
               to the attention of the court
               the fact that our client
               was 20 years old
               when he was ordered
               to camp duty
               As witnesses have substantiated

our client had keen intellectual interests
and his whole personality
made him utterly unfit
for the task assigned him
We would like to call attention to the fact
that one year after completing
his secondary schooling
our client
was granted a further period of leave
to study law
In the last year of the war
he was wounded in front-line action
Immediately after the war
as soon as he was able to settle down
in more normal conditions
he went on to develop in exemplary fashion
He studied agriculture
passed his assessor's examination
was an expert
with the Economic Advisory Council
and until his arrest
was an instructor
in an agricultural school

PROSECUTING
ATTORNEY: Accused Stark
              did you take part in the first gassings
              which were carried out
              on Soviet prisoners of war
              in the first weeks of September 1941

ACCUSED #12:No
PROSECUTING
ATTORNEY: Large-scale extermination
              of Soviet prisoners of war began
              in the fall and winter of 1941
              These resulted in the death of 25,000 men

You processed these prisoners
You knew of their death
you consented to their death
and you performed
essential parts of the operation

COUNSEL FOR
THE DEFENSE: We strongly protest
these attacks on our client
Such wholesale accusations
are completely meaningless
Only clear-cut proofs of criminal acts
or conspiracy in committing such acts
in relation to the charges of murder
are relevant to these proceedings
Wherever there is the slightest doubt
the benefit must be given to the accused
*[The Accused laugh nodding in
agreement]*

THE SONG OF S.S. CORPORAL STARK

III

JUDGE: Accused Stark
you never once took part in the gassings

ACCUSED #12: There was one time I had to

JUDGE: How many prisoners were involved

ACCUSED #12: Somewhere around 150
Four truckloads anyway

JUDGE: Who were the prisoners

ACCUSED #12: It was a mixed transport

JUDGE: What was your job

ACCUSED #12: I stood outside by the stairs
after I had led them
into the crematorium
The medical orderlies
in charge of the gassing
had locked the doors
and were making the necessary preparations

JUDGE: What kind of preparations

ACCUSED #12: They got out the cans
and put on their gas masks
Then they went up the embankment

154

to the roof deck
Usually it took four men to do the job
This time there were only three
and they called back
they needed somebody to help them out
Since I was the only one around
Grabner said
Move
give them a hand
Then the camp leader came over
and said rather sharply
If you don't go up there
in you go
So I had to go up
and help pour

JUDGE: Where was the gas thrown in

ACCUSED #12:Through vents in the deck

JUDGE: What did the people in the chamber below
                do then

ACCUSED #12:I don't know

JUDGE: You didn't hear anything
                of what was going on down there

ACCUSED #12:They screamed

JUDGE: For how long

ACCUSED #12:Around 10 or 15 minutes

JUDGE: Who opened the chamber afterward

ACCUSED #12: One of the orderlies

JUDGE: What did you see in there

ACCUSED #12: I didn't take a very close look

JUDGE: Did you see anything wrong
with what you saw there

ACCUSED #12: No
not at all
Only the way it was done

JUDGE: What do you mean

ACCUSED #12: If they had been shot
it would have been one thing
But the use of gas
was unmanly and cowardly

JUDGE: Accused Stark
during the course of your duties
didn't you ever have any doubts
about your conduct in the camp

ACCUSED #12: Your Honor
I would like to explain that
Every third word we heard
even back in grammar school
was about
how they
were to blame for everything
and how they
ought to be weeded out
It was hammered into us
that this would only be for the good

of our people
In leadership school
we were taught above all
to accept everything
without question
If anybody did raise a question
they were told
What is being done
is done strictly according to the law
It's no use saying
the laws are different now
We were told
You've got to study
You've got to have an education
It's more important than food
Your Honor
we weren't supposed to think for ourselves
There were others around
to do our thinking for us
    [*Assenting laughter from the Accused*]

END OF PART I

THE SONG OF THE BLACK WALL

I

3RD WITNESS: Executions were
carried out in front of the Black Wall
in the yard of Barrack 11

JUDGE: Where was Barrack 11

3RD WITNESS: At the far right end
of the old camp

JUDGE: Can the witness
describe the yard

3RD WITNESS: It was between Barrack 10 and Barrack 11
and took up a whole barrack length
about 40 yards
It was closed off at both ends
by brick walls

JUDGE: How did one enter the yard

3RD WITNESS: Through a side door from Barrack 11
or through the gate in the front brick wall

JUDGE: Was there any way of seeing into the yard

3RD WITNESS: Only through the ground-floor windows
at the front of Barrack 11
When the gate was opened
to remove the dead

158

there was a curfew
All the other windows in Barrack 11
were bricked up except for a crack at the top
Windows in the women's barrack
on the other side
were boarded up

JUDGE: How high was the wall

3RD WITNESS: About 14 feet high

JUDGE: And where was the Black Wall

3RD WITNESS: Opposite the front gate
against the back wall

JUDGE: What did the Black Wall look like

3RD WITNESS: It was made out of thick planks
covered with tarred canvas
Bullet-proof walls
came out at an angle from the back

JUDGE: How large was the Black Wall

3RD WITNESS: About 10 feet high
13 wide

JUDGE: From where were sentenced prisoners
brought out to the Black Wall

3RD WITNESS: They came out through the side door
of Barrack 11

JUDGE: Describe the procedure

3RD WITNESS: The Bunker-Jakob led out
two prisoners at a time
The prisoners were naked

JUDGE: Who was this Bunker-Jakob

3RD WITNESS: He was the special-duty prisoner
assigned to Barrack 11
He was a big powerfully built man
a former boxer

JUDGE: How were the prisoners brought out

3RD WITNESS: Jakob was in the middle
holding them by the arm

JUDGE: Were the prisoners' hands bound

3RD WITNESS: Up until 1942 they were
tied behind the back with wire
Later they stopped using it
since experience showed that most prisoners
went along quietly

JUDGE: How far was it from the side door
to the Black Wall

3RD WITNESS: First the six steps down from the door
then 20 paces to the Black Wall
Everything went at the double
When Jakob had brought
the prisoners to the wall
he ran back
to get the next two

JUDGE: How were the executions carried out

3RD WITNESS: Prisoners were put
face to the wall
three to six feet apart
The executioner went up to the first one
put his gun against the prisoner's neck
then fired from about four inches off
The other prisoner saw it
As soon as the first had fallen
it was his turn

JUDGE: What kind of weapon
was used

3RD WITNESS: A small-caliber rifle with a silencer

JUDGE: Whom did you see
at the Black Wall executions

3RD WITNESS: The camp commander
the adjutant
the head of the Political Division Grabner
and his assistants
Among others I saw Broad Stark
Boger and Schlage
Kaduk was frequently there too

COUNSEL FOR
THE DEFENSE: Are you sure
the adjutant was there

3RD WITNESS: He was a familiar figure
We knew the camp commander
We knew his adjutant just as well

COUNSEL FOR
THE DEFENSE: During the executions
what were your duties in the yard

3RD WITNESS: As a medical student
I was assigned to the corpse-bearers' detail

JUDGE: Which of the accused
took part in the executions

3RD WITNESS: Boger Broad Stark Schlage and Kaduk
I saw them carry out executions on their own

JUDGE: Accused Boger
did you take part in executions
carried out at the Black Wall

ACCUSED #2: I never fired a shot in the camp

JUDGE: Accused Broad
did you take part in executions
carried out at the Black Wall

ACCUSED #16: I was never required to carry out
such assignments

JUDGE: Accused Schlage
as supervisor of Barrack 11
did you
take part in executions
carried out at the Black Wall

ACCUSED #14: I was not authorized to do so

JUDGE: Accused Kaduk
did you take part in executions
carried out at the Black Wall

ACCUSED #7: I never set foot in Barrack 11
What has been said here about me
is nothing but a lie

JUDGE: Can the witness tell us
                    if death sentences
                    were read out before the executions

3RD WITNESS: Not usually
                    When there was a death sentence
                    a special execution squad appeared
                    but I can only recall that happening
                    in a few cases
                    Generally prisoners were
                    just hauled out of the cells in Barrack 11

JUDGE: What condition were the prisoners in

3RD WITNESS: Most of them were badly injured
                    after the interrogations
                    and after their time in the Bunker
                    Some
                    had to be carried out to the Wall
                    on stretchers

JUDGE: We call as witness
                    the then ranking officer
                    of the accused here present
                    As head of the Central Office
                    of the Security Police attached to the camp
                    and presiding officer at its summary court
                    what did you have to do
                    with the executions carried out
                    by the Political Division

1ST WITNESS: My post had no connection whatsoever
                    with the functioning
                    of the Political Division within the camp
                    I dealt exclusively with cases
                    relating to partisan resistance

These were brought over to the camp
and trial was held there in a hearing room

JUDGE: Where was this room

1ST WITNESS: In one of the barracks

JUDGE: Was it not in Barrack 11

1ST WITNESS: That's more than I can remember

6TH WITNESS: I was the clerk in Barrack 11
My job gave me an idea
of the working of the summary courts
Court sessions were held in a room
on the front left side of Barrack 11

JUDGE: What was the room like

6TH WITNESS: There were four windows onto the courtyard
and a long table

JUDGE: Do you recall this room

1ST WITNESS: No

JUDGE: Did you ever go into the inner area
of the old camp

1ST WITNESS: That's more than I can remember

JUDGE: Did you ever pass through the camp gate

1ST WITNESS: It's possible
I remember a band
playing there once

JUDGE: Were you never in the yard of Barrack 11

1ST WITNESS: Once perhaps
There was said to be a wall there
I can't remember it though

JUDGE: But surely a black wall
is very noticeable

1ST WITNESS: I have no recollection of it

JUDGE: You were
the presiding officer
at these summary sessions
Did the defendant have counsel

1ST WITNESS: If it was requested

JUDGE: Was it ever requested

1ST WITNESS: Rarely

JUDGE: And when it was

1ST WITNESS: Then counsel was provided

JUDGE: Who was the defense

1ST WITNESS: Somebody from the office staff

JUDGE: Were intensive interrogations
ever employed

1ST WITNESS: There was never any need for that
At least I personally never
heard of any such interrogations

The facts of the case were so clear
there was no need
for intensive interrogation

JUDGE: What were the facts of the case

1ST WITNESS: They were exclusively
                cases of treasonable activity

JUDGE: Did the prisoners confess

1ST WITNESS: There was nothing to deny

JUDGE: How were these confessions obtained

1ST WITNESS: By means of interrogations

JUDGE: Who conducted the interrogations

1ST WITNESS: The Political Division

JUDGE: As a judge
                were you ever troubled
                about how these confessions
                were obtained

1ST WITNESS: What can I do
                if one or another of my people
                exceeds his authority
                I strictly and repeatedly
                enjoined my assistants
                that they were to conduct
                themselves correctly
                at all hearings

JUDGE: Were witnesses called at interrogations

166

1ST WITNESS:	Not as a rule
	We asked if everything was as stated
	and they all said yes

JUDGE:	Then you only had to deliver death sentences

1ST WITNESS:	Yes
	There were practically no acquittals
	Proceedings were instituted only
	when everything was perfectly clear

JUDGE:	Did you ever notice
	any marks on the accused
	which might have indicated improper treat-ment

1ST WITNESS:	No

JUDGE:	Were women and children
	executed at the Black Wall

1ST WITNESS:	I know nothing about that

6TH WITNESS:	Among the prisoners
	brought into the barrack
	to be sentenced by the court
	there were many women and children
	The indictment was for smuggling
	or for contact with partisan groups
	In contrast to the camp prisoners
	who were locked up in the basement
	prisoners arrested by the Security Police
	were held on the ground floor of Barrack 11
	They were taken into the session room
	one by one
	The judge read the sentence

He only read out the names and then said
You have been sentenced to death
Most of the prisoners sentenced
didn't understand the language
and had no idea
why they had been arrested
From the courtroom
they were immediately taken
to the washroom
where they were told to undress
and from there
out to the courtyard

PROSECUTING
ATTORNEY: As judge of the summary court
how many sentences were you
called upon to deliver

1ST WITNESS: I cannot remember that
PROSECUTING
ATTORNEY: How often
were your sessions held

1ST WITNESS: I can't recall
PROSECUTING
ATTORNEY: How long
did a session of the summary court last

1ST WITNESS: I couldn't say
PROSECUTING
ATTORNEY: You are at present the director
of a large business concern
As such you must certainly be accustomed
to dealing with large numbers
and complex time calculations
How many people
did you sentence

1ST WITNESS: I don't know

6TH WITNESS: At a single session of the summary court
an average of 100 to 150 death sentences
was delivered
The session lasted
an hour and a half to two hours
and took place every two weeks

PROSECUTING
ATTORNEY: How many prisoners
all told
would the witness estimate
were shot at the Black Wall

6TH WITNESS: The death books and our own notes
show
that together
with the usual Bunker clearings
approximately 20,000 people
were shot at the Black Wall

THE SONG OF THE BLACK WALL

II

7TH WITNESS: Early one morning
in the fall of 1943
I saw a little girl
in the courtyard of Barrack 11
She wore a red dress
and her hair was braided into a long pigtail
She stood alone
her hands at her sides
like a soldier
She bent over once
to dust her shoes off
and then stood still again
Then I saw Boger come into the courtyard
He kept his gun
hidden behind his back
He took the child by the hand
and she went along with him like a good girl
and let him stand her
face to the wall
against the Black Wall
The child looked around once more
Boger turned her face to the wall
lifted his gun
and shot her

COUNSEL FOR
THE DEFENSE: How could the witness have seen this

7TH WITNESS: I was cleaning the washroom
which was next to the door
leading out to the yard

JUDGE: How old was the child

7TH WITNESS: Six or seven years old
The corpse-bearers told me later
that the girl's parents
had been shot there a few days before

ACCUSED #2: Your Honor
I never shot a child
I never shot anyone at all

3RD WITNESS: I saw Boger by the Black Wall many times
I can still hear him yelling
Head up
and then shooting the prisoner in the neck

JUDGE: Isn't it possible that the witness
may be confusing Boger with someone else

3RD WITNESS: We all knew Boger
and the way he waddled when he walked
We used to see him frequently
riding to Barrack 11 on his bicycle
his gun slung over his shoulder
Sometimes he used to pull prisoners
along behind him
like dogs on a leash

JUDGE: Accused Boger
would you care to reconsider
your statement
that you never fired a shot in the camp

ACCUSED #2: I stand by my statement today
and a thousand years from now
I will still stand by it

Not that I would have been afraid to shoot
I would only have been carrying out orders

3RD WITNESS: Executions were carried out
every Wednesday and Friday
On May 14 1943
I saw Boger
kill 17 prisoners
I made a note of the date
because my friend Berger was one of them
He had already been beaten to a pulp
on the swing
Berger shouted
You murderers you criminals
then Boger shot him
Another prisoner was on his knees
in front of Boger
Boger shot him in the face
When word passed around
Boger's here
we knew what it meant
We called him
the Black Death

ACCUSED #2: I've had a lot of nicknames besides that one
We all had nicknames
That doesn't prove anything

JUDGE: Accused Boger
during the course of this trial
witnesses have repeatedly testified
that you
killed people in the camp
Has all this testimony
in your opinion
simply been invented

ACCUSED #2: I was frequently
            present at executions
            Most likely
            the witnesses are confusing me
            with somebody else
            They've got Boger
            so what do they do
            It's natural
            They dump all their hate on me

JUDGE: You didn't shoot once

ACCUSED #2: I did
            once

JUDGE: You did shoot once

ACCUSED #2: It was an exception
            I was ordered
            to take part in an execution

JUDGE: How did that happen

ACCUSED #2: At one of the Bunker clearings
            Grabner called out the order
            Sergeant Boger
            will carry on with the shooting

JUDGE: How many times did you shoot

ACCUSED #2: Twice
            on that one single occasion
            Later I refused
            to take part in such things
            I said
            Either I work here

or I work with Identification
I can't
do both jobs at the same time

JUDGE: Who were the people
you had to shoot

ACCUSED #2: They belonged to a transport
that hadn't been processed
by Identification

JUDGE: That means
it was assumed from the start
they were going to die

ACCUSED #2: I believe so

JUDGE: Accused Boger
why have you consistently maintained
up until this very moment
that no one in the camp
met his death at your hand

ACCUSED #2: Your Honor
when you get so much thrown at you
you just can't commit yourself right off

JUDGE: And you persist in maintaining
that you shot in only two cases
and that no one ever died
as a result
of intensive interrogations

ACCUSED #2: Yes
On my sacred word of honor

JUDGE: As one of the corpse-bearers' detail
when were you required to appear
in the courtyard of Barrack 11

3RD WITNESS: We were called up
about an hour before the execution

JUDGE: Where were you stationed

3RD WITNESS: In the Ambulance Barrack

JUDGE: Where was that

3RD WITNESS: Across from the Bunker Barrack
on the front right side of the camp

JUDGE: How were you alerted for duty

3RD WITNESS: A clerk ran in from Barrack 11
He shouted
Corpse-bearers
one stretcher
two stretchers
If he called for one stretcher we knew
it would be a small execution
If he called for more
it was a big one

JUDGE: Where did the clerk stand

3RD WITNESS: He stayed out in the corridor
and we ran out to him
When he told us
how many were needed
the Kapo
picked out the ones to go

JUDGE: Where did you have to go then

3RD WITNESS: When the siren had signaled the curfew
                       we went out into the courtyard
                       through the door in Barrack 11
                       We had to line up next to the door
                       and stand there with our stretchers ready

JUDGE: What sort of stretchers were they

3RD WITNESS: Canvas
                       with wood shafts
                       and metal legs

JUDGE: Was a doctor present

3RD WITNESS: Only for big executions
                       Otherwise just the officers
                       of the Political Division

JUDGE: Where were prisoners awaiting execution kept

3RD WITNESS: They were held in the washroom
                       and in the hall outside

JUDGE: What preparations preceded the execution

3RD WITNESS: After prisoners came up from the cellar
                       they had to take off their clothes
                       in the washroom
                       or out in the hall
                       Numbers were written on their chests
                       with indelible pencil
                       A prisoner clerk checked out the numbers
                       then crossed them out

as prisoners
were taken out to the yard

JUDGE: What order was given
to bring out the prisoners

3RD WITNESS: The order was
Take off
Then the Bunker-Jakob ran out
with the first two
As soon as they stood against the wall
we too got the order
Take off
and we ran out with our stretcher

JUDGE: Who gave the order

3RD WITNESS: Either the doctor
or one of the officers

JUDGE: Had the prisoners already been shot
when you got there

3RD WITNESS: Usually the first one had fallen
and the second fell right after
But sometimes it took longer
Then we stood behind
the executioner

JUDGE: Why did it sometimes take longer

3RD WITNESS: Occasionally a gun jammed
And we'd wait while the man
took care of it

JUDGE: How did the prisoners
                        who were to be executed behave

3RD WITNESS: Some prayed
                        others sang national
                        or religious songs
                        Once though
                        when a woman started to scream
                        I heard the order
                        Get that crazy one first

JUDGE: How did you remove the dead

3RD WITNESS: As soon as they had dropped in the sand
                        in front of the wall
                        we picked them up by the hands and feet
                        laid the first one face up on the stretcher
                        the second one face down and reversed
                        so he lay with his face
                        between the legs of the one underneath
                        Then we ran to the drainage ditch
                        and tipped them out

JUDGE: Where was this ditch

3RD WITNESS: Along the left edge of the courtyard

JUDGE: What happened then

3RD WITNESS: While we ran with the stretcher
                        over to the ditch
                        the Bunker-Jakob was already running
                        the next two
                        out to the wall
                        and the two other bearers ran
                        behind him with their stretcher

We laid the dead down in layers
on top of each other
with their heads over the ditch
so the blood could drain off

JUDGE: Did the prisoners die
              immediately after execution

3RD WITNESS: Sometimes the bullet
              only went in through an ear
              or through the chin
              and they were still alive
              when they were carried off
              Then we had to put the stretcher down
              and the injured would be shot again
              this time in the head
              The Arrest Supervisor Schlage
              always took another look
              at the bodies we had dumped
              and if any of them still moved
              he had him pulled out of the heap
              and finished off the kill
              Once Schlage said to one
              who was still living
              Get up
              I saw
              the man try to pull himself up
              Then Schlage said
              Stay down
              and shot him in the heart
              and in both temples
              But the man was still alive
              I don't know how many more he got
              First
              one in the throat
              The blood that came out was black

Schlage said
That one has as many lives as a cat

JUDGE: Accused Schlage
have you anything to say to this

ACCUSED #14:It's a riddle to me
To that
I wouldn't know what to say

THE SONG OF THE BLACK WALL
III

7TH WITNESS: I saw Schlage in the washroom once
with a family that had been brought in
The father had to get down and duck-walk
and then Schlage shot him in the head
Then it was the child's turn
and after that the mother
He had to shoot the child more than once
It screamed and didn't die right away

COUNSEL FOR
THE DEFENSE: Why did he shoot them in the washroom
when the Execution Wall
was just outside

7TH WITNESS: Smaller executions
were often carried out in the washroom
because it was simpler
The showers could be turned on
to wash the blood off the floor

COUNSEL FOR
THE DEFENSE: Describe the washroom

7TH WITNESS: It was a small room with one window
that was covered over with a blanket
The bottom half of the room was tarred
the upper half painted white
There were thick black pipes in the corners
About six feet up
a pipe with shower heads
crossed through the middle of the room

JUDGE: Accused Schlage
                do you still maintain
                that you shot nobody in the camp

ACCUSED #14: I emphatically deny
                these accusations
                I never took part in any killings

7TH WITNESS: Some of the corpses
                brought into the washroom
                had flesh cut out of them

JUDGE: What do you mean by that

7TH WITNESS: In the summer of 1944
                I saw the first of those mutilated corpses
                A man was unloaded
                whom I had already noticed
                when he stripped for execution
                He was a giant
                I saw him lying in the washroom
                There were men in white coats
                and with surgical instruments
                standing around him
                Flesh had been cut out of his stomach
                At first we thought
                he must have swallowed something
                and they were getting it out
                but later on it happened more often
                that flesh was cut out of corpses
                Afterwards it was mainly the case
                with bodies of the stronger heavier women

3RD WITNESS: Once we had to remove
                the corpses of 70 women
                Their breasts were gone

and there were deep cuts
in their abdomens and thighs
The medical orderlies loaded
potfuls of human flesh
into the sidecar of a motorcycle
On the wagon
we had to cover up
the corpses with boards

4TH WITNESS: In Experimental Research Barrack 10
I looked through a crack in the window boards
I saw the corpses down in the courtyard
We had heard a loud hum
It was swarms of flies
The ground was covered with blood
Then I saw
the executioners walking across the courtyard
smoking and laughing
[*Points at the Accused*]

COUNSEL FOR
THE DEFENSE: We cannot allow
these insults to our clients
to pass unchallenged
We want the record
to show our objection
[*The Accused express their indignation*]

THE SONG OF PHENOL

I

8TH WITNESS: I charge Medical Orderly Klehr
with the singlehanded killing
of thousands of prisoners
by injecting phenol into the heart

ACCUSED #9: That is slander
Only in a very few cases
was I compelled to supervise injections
and then
only with the greatest reluctance

8TH WITNESS: At least 30 prisoners were killed
daily in the infirmary
Sometimes as many as 200

JUDGE: Where were these injections given

8TH WITNESS: In the Contagious Diseases Barrack nearby
That was Barrack 20

JUDGE: Where was Barrack 20

8TH WITNESS: It was the next to the last building
on the right-hand side
of the center barrack row
The last building in that row was 21
the camp infirmary
As a prisoner attendant I had to
take selected prisoners

across the yard
to the Contagious Diseases Barrack

JUDGE: Was this yard closed off

8TH WITNESS: Only by low iron railings at each end

JUDGE: How were the prisoners transferred

8TH WITNESS: Those able to walk
crossed the courtyard half naked
They held their blanket and wooden shoes
over their heads
Many patients had to be supported
or carried over
They entered Barrack 20
through the side door

JUDGE: In which room
were the injections given

8TH WITNESS: In Room 1
That was the doctor's office
It was at the end of the central corridor

JUDGE: Where did the prisoners wait

8TH WITNESS: They had to line up in the corridor
The critically ill lay on the floor
Prisoners went into the room two by two
Dr Entress assigned Klehr
a third of the patients
That wasn't enough for him
When Dr Entress had left for the day
Klehr stayed to make additional selections

JUDGE: You saw this yourself

8TH WITNESS: Yes
                    I saw it
                    Klehr loved round numbers
                    If the final count didn't satisfy him
                    he went through the wards
                    selecting victims to round off the number
                    He looked over the fever charts
                    which under his supervision
                    were meticulously kept
                    then made his selections accordingly

JUDGE: What were the round numbers
                    that Klehr especially favored

8TH WITNESS: From about 23 on
                    he would round it off to 30
                    from 36 to 40
                    and so on
                    He ordered selected patients
                    to get up and follow him

JUDGE: What order was given

8TH WITNESS: You come along
                    you come along
                    you come along
                    and you

ACCUSED #9:   Your Honor
                    this statement is untrue
                    I was not authorized to make selections

JUDGE: What were your duties then

ACCUSED #9: I only had to see to it
that the right prisoners were brought over

JUDGE: And what did you
have to do when injections were given

ACCUSED #9: That's something I'd like to know myself
I just stood around
The treatment
was carried out by special-duty prisoners
I kept away from that
I wasn't going to let those
contaminated prisoners
breathe in my face

JUDGE: As staff orderly
what were your duties

ACCUSED #9: I was responsible
(a) for discipline and sanitation
(b) for registration
(c) for the patients' nutrition

JUDGE: What was their diet

ACCUSED #9: In the dietetic kitchen milk-soup was
prepared for post-operational patients

JUDGE: How many patients were in the infirmary

ACCUSED #9: On the average some
500 to 600 patients

JUDGE: What were the accommodations

ACCUSED #9: They lay on triple-decker bunks

JUDGE: How were they registered

ACCUSED #9:   Every sick-report received
                     was card-indexed
                     Selections among advanced patients
                     were then registered

JUDGE: What were advanced patients

ACCUSED #9:   Prisoners
                     whose state of health was critical

JUDGE: How were the selections made

ACCUSED #9:   The camp doctor examined the prisoner
                     and the index card with the diagnosis
                     If he did not return the card
                     to the prisoner doctor
                     but gave it to the prisoner clerk instead
                     it meant
                     the prisoner was to receive the injection

JUDGE: What happened then

ACCUSED #9:   The cards were assembled on a table
                     and processed

JUDGE: What does processed mean

ACCUSED #9:   The prisoner clerk had
                     to compile a list from the cards on hand
                     This list was then handed over
                     to the medical orderly
                     In accordance with this list
                     patients were dispatched

9TH WITNESS: On Christmas 1942
Klehr walked into the ward
and said
Today
I am camp doctor
Today
I shall take care
of the advanced patients
With the stem of his pipe
he pointed out 40 of them
and designated them for injection
After Christmas
a requisition for special rations
was put in
for Medical Orderly Klehr
I saw the requisition
It said
For Special Treatment
carried out 24 12 1942
a half-pint brandy
5 cigarettes 3½ ounces sausage
is requested

ACCUSED #9: That's ridiculous
I had home leave every Christmas
My wife can testify to that

JUDGE: Accused Klehr
do you still maintain
you had no part whatsoever
in selections and killings
by means of phenol injection

ACCUSED #9: All I had to do
was supervise standard operating procedures

JUDGE: Did you always find
          these procedures justified

ACCUSED #9:   In the beginning I was astonished
          when I heard
          that patients were injected
          by special-duty prisoners
          But then I realized
          that the patients were incurable
          and endangered the health of the entire camp

JUDGE: How were the injections given

ACCUSED #9:   Special-duty prisoner Peter Werl
          from the Ambulance Barrack
          and another called Felix
          administered the injections
          At first
          they were injected into a vein in the arm
          However due to the undernourished
          condition of the prisoners
          these veins were hard to find
          For that reason phenol was later on
          injected directly into the heart
          The hypo wasn't even empty
          the man was already dead

JUDGE: Did you ever refuse
          to be present at these sessions

ACCUSED #9:   I would have been put up against the wall

JUDGE: You never expressed your misgivings
          to the camp doctor

ACCUSED #9:   I did

a number of times
But all I was told was
I had my duty to do

JUDGE: Couldn't you have arranged
for a transfer to some other post

ACCUSED #9: Mr President
we were all in a strait jacket
We were nothing but numbers
just like the prisoners
With us
a man began to count for something
only when he had a degree
We should have just dared try
to question anything

JUDGE: Were you never compelled
to give an injection yourself

ACCUSED #9: Once when I started to complain
the camp doctor said
In the future you'll do it yourself

JUDGE: And then you did undertake
selections and killings

ACCUSED #9: In a few cases
yes
I was compelled to

JUDGE: How often did you give injections

ACCUSED #9: Generally twice a week
to about 12 to 15 men
But I was only there for two or three months

JUDGE: That would come to at least
                200 killed

ACCUSED #9:   It could have been 250 to 300
                I don't remember exactly
                It was orders
                There wasn't anything I could do about it

8TH WITNESS: Medical Orderly Klehr
                participated
                in the killing
                of at least 16,000 prisoners

ACCUSED #9:   That's preposterous
                I'm supposed to have injected away
                16,000 people
                when there were only 16,000
                in the whole camp
                That wouldn't have left anybody but the band
                        [*The Accused laugh*]

THE SONG OF PHENOL

II

JUDGE: Accused Klehr
how did you kill the prisoners

ACCUSED #9: As prescribed by orders
with an injection of phenol in the heart
But I didn't do that all by myself

JUDGE: Who else was there

ACCUSED #9: I don't remember

9TH WITNESS: The accused Scherpe and Hantl
assisted in the killings by phenol
Yet their behavior was very different
from Klehr's
They were polite to us
and said Good morning
when they came into the barrack
and when they left they said
Good afternoon
We often saw Klehr wild with rage
Scherpe
on the other hand
was calm and courteous
He had a pleasant way
of treating people
I never saw Scherpe beat
or kick anybody
Patients who came to him

often had confidence in him
and believed they were only
going to be treated for their illness

JUDGE: As one of the prisoner doctors
in the infirmary
· what can the witness tell us
about the early stages
of phenol injection

9TH WITNESS: It was camp doctor Entress
who initiated the injections
He began by using gasoline
but that proved to be impractical
since it took three quarters of an hour
for the patient to die
A quicker means was sought
The second to be used was hydrogen
After that came phenol

JUDGE: Whom did you see administer
these injections

9TH WITNESS: At first Dr Entress himself
then Scherpe and Hantl
Hantl did it infrequently
We thought of him as a decent person

JUDGE: Did you see
Klehr kill

9TH WITNESS: I did not see it myself
Both Schwarz and Gebhard
the two prisoners who had to hold the victim
during the injection
told me about it

But we didn't waste much time discussing it
It was such an ordinary event

COUNSEL FOR
THE DEFENSE: The witness
mentions different names
in connection
with these special-duty prisoners
Weren't the prisoners named Werl and Felix

9TH WITNESS: There were many special-duty prisoners
who had to do this job

COUNSEL FOR
THE DEFENSE: And didn't these prisoners
also do the killing

9TH WITNESS: In the beginning they had to
COUNSEL FOR
THE DEFENSE: So the prisoners were killed
by their own people

PROSECUTING
ATTORNEY: We protest
these tactics by which the defense
seeks to blame prisoners
for actions carried out
under the threat of death

COUNSEL FOR
THE DEFENSE: The troops in the camp
were subject to the same threat

PROSECUTING
ATTORNEY: In no instance has it been proved
that anything was done
to those who refused
to take part in killings

COUNSEL FOR
THE DEFENSE: That is easy enough to say now
In the eyes of the law a subordinate

can be held responsible
only when he knows
that the order of his superior
involves the commission of a civil
or military crime
Our clients acted in good faith
and according to the basic principle
of unquestioning execution of their duty
With their oath of allegiance to the death
all submitted to the goals
established by
the then existing administration
as did also
the Department of Justice
and the Army

PROSECUTING
ATTORNEY: We repeat that anyone
who recognized the criminal intent of an order
had the choice
of requesting a transfer
We know
why they did not have themselves transferred
At the front
their own lives would have been endangered
So they stayed
where their enemy was defenseless

JUDGE: The court calls as witness
one of the former
ranking camp doctors
In the course of your duties
did you have anything to do with the accused
Klehr Scherpe and Hantl

2ND WITNESS: I did not come into contact
with these men

JUDGE:	Weren't you their superior
2ND WITNESS:	Their only superior there was the camp headquarters doctor All I did was desk work
JUDGE:	What was your position in the medical profession before being called up for service in the camp
2ND WITNESS:	I was a university professor
JUDGE:	And yet with all your professional training you had only office work to do
2ND WITNESS:	Occasionally I also did some work in pathology
JUDGE:	You selected no prisoners for the accused Klehr
2ND WITNESS:	I refused to do so
JUDGE:	You were never present during selections
2ND WITNESS:	Only to accompany the doctor on duty
PROSECUTING ATTORNEY:	Are you aware that those who took part in such actions were granted special rations
2ND WITNESS:	I find it understandable and natural that for the hard work they had to do the men should receive special rations of cigarettes

and brandy
After all it was wartime
Brandy and cigarettes were hard to come by
so of course the men were after them
They saved up their coupons
and then went over with their bottle

PROSECUTING
ATTORNEY: You too

2ND WITNESS: Yes
Everybody went over

PROSECUTING
ATTORNEY: What was your attitude
in regard to the selections

COUNSEL FOR
THE DEFENSE: We object to this question
This witness has already
served his sentence
and he cannot be tried here again

2ND WITNESS: I consider myself
innocent even today
The only patients chosen
were those who couldn't have recovered
anyway

PROSECUTING
ATTORNEY: With your medical training
you saw no alternative

2ND WITNESS: Not with the way things were then
On the front thousands of our own soldiers
were bleeding to death
and people were suffering
in the bombed-out cities

PROSECUTING
ATTORNEY: But we are talking here

of people who
though they had committed no crime
were held under arrest
and murdered
You must have been aware of that

2ND WITNESS: There was nothing I could do about it
My first day there
the army doctor said to me
We're in the asshole of the world here
and we have to behave accordingly

PROSECUTING
ATTORNEY: Were you present
when injections were given

2ND WITNESS: Yes
I had to go in there occasionally

PROSECUTING
ATTORNEY: What did you see there

2ND WITNESS: Klehr put on a doctor's coat
and said to a girl
You have heart trouble
You have to have an injection
Then he jabbed it in
and I ran out

PROSECUTING
ATTORNEY: Was Klehr alone

2ND WITNESS: Yes
PROSECUTING
ATTORNEY: Wasn't the woman held down

2ND WITNESS: No

PROSECUTING
ATTORNEY: The court is in possession of the diary
               you kept during your time in the camp
               In this diary we read
               For lunch today
               roast hare
               a thick leg of mutton
               with potato dumplings and cabbage
               It goes on to say
               Six women injected by Klehr

2ND WITNESS: I must have heard that somewhere
PROSECUTING
ATTORNEY: We read further
               Bicycle trip
               wonderful weather
               Then
               Present at 11 executions
               Three women begged for their lives
               Fresh samples taken from liver
               spleen and pancreas
               following injections of pilocarpin
               What does that mean

2ND WITNESS: I had orders
               to perform autopsies
               The purpose of this work
               was purely scientific
               I had nothing to do with the killings
PROSECUTING
ATTORNEY: The people whose flesh you took
               had you picked them for autopsy
               while they were still alive
COUNSEL FOR
THE DEFENSE: We object
               and remind the prosecution once again

that this witness has already
paid his penalty

PROSECUTING
ATTORNEY: Why did you use human flesh
for your research

2ND WITNESS: Because the guards
ate the beef and horse meat
received
for use in our bacteriological research

JUDGE: Where was the phenol
used for injections
stored

3RD WITNESS: It was stored in the dispensary

JUDGE: Where was the dispensary

3RD WITNESS: In the maintenance buildings outside the camp

JUDGE: Who was in charge of the dispensary

3RD WITNESS: Dr Capesius

JUDGE: Who came for the phenol

3RD WITNESS: The requisition
written up by Klehr
was handed over
to Dr Capesius in the dispensary
by a messenger from the infirmary
The messenger was then given the phenol

JUDGE: Accused Dr Capesius
what do you have to say to this

ACCUSED #3: I don't know anything
about such requisitions

JUDGE: Did you know that people in the camp
were killed by injections of phenol

ACCUSED #3: I heard about it for the first time
just now

JUDGE: Did you store phenol in your dispensary

ACCUSED #3: I never saw any great amount of it there

3RD WITNESS: The phenol was stored in a yellow cupboard
in the corner of the prescription room
Later on there were also big bottles of it
in the cellar

COUNSEL FOR
THE DEFENSE: How does the witness
happen to know this

3RD WITNESS: I was assigned to duty in the dispensary
I saw the new requisition forms
They had been filled out
and signed by Dr Capesius
They called it purified phenol
But I'm not sure whether
the words PRO INJECTIONE were on the forms
too or not

JUDGE: What quantities were requisitioned

3RD WITNESS: Small amounts at first
Later
from 4½ to 11 pounds a month

JUDGE: How is phenol
generally used as a medication

3RD WITNESS: Mixed with glycerine
it is used for ear drops

ACCUSED #3: That's precisely what the phenol in my keeping
was intended for

JUDGE: 4½ to 11 pounds of phenol per month
16 ounces per pound
each ounce containing hundreds of drops
You could have cured the ears
of an entire army
[*The Accused laugh*]
Accused Capesius
do you still maintain
that in your dispensary you never saw
phenol for injection

ACCUSED #3: I neither saw large quantities
of phenol
nor knew
that people were being killed with it

JUDGE: Who received the phenol
obtained from the dispensary

3RD WITNESS: The doctor on duty
He then passed it on to the orderly
in the doctor's office

THE SONG OF PHENOL

III

JUDGE: Describe the doctor's office

6TH WITNESS: It was painted white
             The windows on the courtyard side
             were whitewashed over

JUDGE: How was the room furnished

6TH WITNESS: There were a few cupboards and closets
             and then there was the curtain
             that divided the room

JUDGE: What sort of curtain was it

6TH WITNESS: It was about six feet long
             and it hung from a little below the ceiling
             It was greenish-gray
             The clerk who sat in front of it
             crossed off the patients
             as they were brought in

JUDGE: What was behind the curtain

6TH WITNESS: A small table
             and a couple of stools
             On the wall
             there were rubber aprons
             and pink rubber gloves
             hanging on hooks

COUNSEL FOR
THE DEFENSE: How does the witness
know this

6TH WITNESS: I was a corpse-bearer
We sat in the washroom right next
to the doctor's room
The door was open
and we could see everything

JUDGE: What happened to the prisoners
who were to be given
the phenol injection

6TH WITNESS: They were brought in two at a time
from the corridor
One of the two special-duty prisoners
who stood ready behind the curtain
held one prisoner
while the injection was given
The other one had to wait
on the other side of the curtain
Meanwhile the second special-duty prisoner
had filled the hypodermic

JUDGE: What kind of syringe was used

6TH WITNESS: At first
when they gave intravenous injections
they were syringes with a capacity of five cc's
Later
when injections were made
directly into the heart
they used syringes that held only two cc's
They were fitted with needles

generally used for making lumbar punctures
A supply of syringes was kept in a pouch

JUDGE: In what sort of vessel was
the phenol kept

6TH WITNESS: In a bottle
similar to a thermos
The phenol was poured out
into a small basin
The syringes were filled from this
The fluid turned red
because needles were seldom changed
and they were bloody from the injections

JUDGE: Did the patients know
what was going to happen to them

6TH WITNESS: Most of them did not
They were told
they were going to be inoculated

JUDGE: They allowed
this to be done to them

6TH WITNESS: Most of them did as they were told
Many were in a state of utter exhaustion

JUDGE: Whom did you see administer injections

6TH WITNESS: Klehr took the syringe
when it had been filled
He wore a rubber apron
rubber gloves and high rubber boots
The sleeves of his white coat
were rolled up

JUDGE:	What happened to the prisoner then

6TH WITNESS:	If he still had a shirt on
	he had to take it off
	and sit down on the stool
	He had to hold his left arm up
	and out to the side
	and cover his mouth with his hand
	That was to smother the scream
	and to leave the heart open
	The two special-duty prisoners
	held him down

JUDGE:	What were their names

6TH WITNESS:	They were called Schwarz and Weiss
	Schwarz held the prisoner
	by the shoulders
	Weiss kept the prisoner's hand
	against his mouth
	and Klehr jabbed the needle
	into his heart

JUDGE:	Did death occur immediately

6TH WITNESS:	Most of them made a faint sound
	as if they were exhaling
	Generally they were dead then
	The death rattle went on in some of them
	and stopped only
	after they had been taken off
	to the washroom
	Some were still in their death agony
	when we took them off
	The rest were dragged out
	with a leather thong

we slipped around their wrists
It went very quickly
Often two or three patients
were finished off
inside a minute

JUDGE: What happened to those
who were still alive
after the injection

6TH WITNESS: I remember a man
who was tall and powerfully built
He got up to his feet in the washroom
with the injection in his heart
I remember it very clearly
There was a boiler
and next to it a bench
Holding on to the boiler
and the bench
he pulled himself up
Then Klehr came in
and gave him a second injection
Others were sometimes only unconscious
because the needle hadn't gone into the heart
and the phenol had entered the lung
When he was done for the day
Klehr always went into the washroom
to look over the stacked-up bodies
If one of them was still alive
he shot him in the back of the neck
Or sometimes he would just say
This one won't make it to the crematorium

JUDGE: Did it ever happen that living prisoners
were taken out with the dead

6TH WITNESS: Sometimes
yes

JUDGE: And they were burned alive

6TH WITNESS: Yes
Or killed with a shovel
at the ovens

JUDGE: Did prisoners ever
resist

6TH WITNESS: Once there was a loud shout
This is what I saw
The two special-duty prisoners
were sitting on top of a bare-chested man
who was smeared all over with blood
The man's head had been split open
A poker was lying on the floor
Klehr stood there
the hypodermic in his hand
Klehr knelt down on top of the man
who was still thrashing violently
and jabbed the needle in

JUDGE: Accused Klehr
what do you have to say to these accusations

ACCUSED #9: I know nothing about the case in question

JUDGE: Do you recognize the witness

ACCUSED #9: Your Honor
This is important
I don't know this witness

and I knew every single prisoner
employed in the corpse-bearer detail

7TH WITNESS: On September 28 1942
it was my father's turn
He was brought in
together with another prisoner
Klehr said to him
You're going to be given
a typhus shot now
He quickly injected both of them
in the heart
He was in a hurry
to get back to his rabbit-breeding
I held my father
and then carried him out myself

JUDGE: Accused Klehr
do you know the witness

ACCUSED #9: That's Weiss
He was weeping at the time
so I asked him why he was weeping
Had he told me
right away that it was his father
I would have let him live

JUDGE: Why didn't you tell him right away

7TH WITNESS: I was scared
Klehr would say
Sit down next to him

JUDGE: Were children among those
killed by injection

7TH WITNESS: Once in the spring of 1943
more than 100 children were killed

JUDGE:	Who carried out this killing
7TH WITNESS:	The killing was carried out by staff orderlies Hantl and Scherpe
JUDGE:	Can the witness provide us with the exact number of children killed at that time
7TH WITNESS:	There were 119 children
JUDGE:	Do you recall the exact date
7TH WITNESS:	It was the 23rd of February
JUDGE:	How do you know this
7TH WITNESS:	I was the clerk at that execution It was my job to cross the children off the list They were boys from 13 to 17 years old Their parents had been shot earlier
JUDGE:	Where did these children come from
7TH WITNESS:	They came from the province of Zamos a region that had been cleared to make room for settlers from the home country
JUDGE:	Accused Scherpe did you take part in this killing
ACCUSED #10:	Mr Chairman I would like to state categorically that I never killed a single person

JUDGE: Accused Hantl
                       what do you have to say

ACCUSED #11: That children were shipped in too
                       is completely new to me
                       Excuse me
                       Mr Scherpe
                       did we ever have anything to do
                       with children

JUDGE: You are not permitted here
                       to put any questions to other accused
                       What we want to know from you
                       is whether you took part
                       in the killings by injection

ACCUSED #11: All I cay say to that
                       is that these accusations are lies

JUDGE: Were you present
                       when the injections were given

ACCUSED #11: At first I refused
                       I said
                       Is it absolutely necessary
                       for me to be around
                       a mess like that
                       Anyway I was only there about
                       eight or ten times

JUDGE: How many were killed
                       the times you were there

ACCUSED #11: Not more than five to eight people
                       Then it was over

7TH WITNESS: Hantl helped
                select the patients
                and he helped kill them
                Injections were given almost daily
                The only day they weren't was Sunday

ACCUSED #11: That really makes me laugh
                I never heard such nonsense in my life
                I simply can't understand
                why this witness
                of all people
                should single me out
                when I was the one who helped him out
                when he had committed sabotage

JUDGE: What had he done

ACCUSED #11: He had stolen sheets
                I always did everything I could
                to help the prisoners
                I managed to get fuel for them
                and radishes too

JUDGE: And you did not take part in the killings

ACCUSED #11: No
                I did not

JUDGE: Will the witness
                resume his report
                concerning the children

7TH WITNESS: The children had been brought
                into the courtyard
                They played out there in the morning
                Somebody had even given them a ball

The prisoners there
knew what was going to happen to them
They gave them the best of whatever they had
The children were hungry and anxious
They said they had been beaten
They asked us over and over
Are we going to be killed
Scherpe and Hantl came in the afternoon
During the hours
in which they carried out this action
Barrack 20 was quiet as the grave

JUDGE: Did the children suspect
what was going to happen

7TH WITNESS: The first ones screamed
Then they were told
they were going to be vaccinated
Then they went in quietly
Only the last ones
started to scream again
because their friends
hadn't come out again
They were brought in to me
two by two
and then went in singly
behind the curtain
The only sound I heard
was the thump
when their heads and bodies
struck the washroom floor
Suddenly Scherpe ran out
I heard him say
I can't any more
He ran off somewhere
Hantl took care of the rest

After that
the rumor spread around camp
Scherpe's had a breakdown

JUDGE: Accused Scherpe
do you have anything to say to this

ACCUSED #10: The report of the witness
seems greatly exaggerated to me
Anyway
I don't recall any of this

PROSECUTING
ATTORNEY: Altogether
how many people
would the witness estimate
were killed by phenol injections

7TH WITNESS: Going by figures in the camp books
as well as by our personal calculations
approximately 30,000 people

THE SONG OF THE BUNKER BLOCK

I

8TH WITNESS: I was sentenced
to 30 times in the standing cell
That meant
punitive hard labor during the day
nights in the standing cell

JUDGE: Why were you sentenced

8TH WITNESS: I went through the food line twice

JUDGE: Where were the standing cells

8TH WITNESS: At the end of the cellar corridor
in Barrack 11
There were four of them

JUDGE: How large was a cell

8TH WITNESS: Three feet square
and about six feet high

JUDGE: Was there a window

8TH WITNESS: No
There was an air hole up in the corner
an inch and a half square
The air shaft went out through the wall
It was closed up on the outside
with a perforated tin lid

JUDGE: And the door

8TH WITNESS: You had to crawl in at the bottom
through a wooden hatchway
about 20 inches high
Outside was an iron gate
that bolted shut

JUDGE: Were you alone in the cell

8TH WITNESS: At first I was alone
The last week
there were four of us standing in there

JUDGE: Were prisoners
there
day and night

8TH WITNESS: That was the usual sentence
The method varied
Some prisoners were fed only
every two or three days
Others weren't fed at all
Those had been sentenced to death
by starvation
My friend Kurt Pachala
died in the adjoining cell
after 15 days
Toward the end he ate his shoes
He died the 14th of January 1943
I remember that
because it was my birthday
A prisoner sentenced to
the standing cell without food
could scream and swear
as much as he wanted

The door was never opened
For the first five nights
he screamed
Then hunger stopped
and thirst took over
He begged
he prayed and he moaned
He drank his urine
and licked the walls
The thirst went on for 13 days
Then no sound came from his cell
It took more than two weeks
for him to die
Corpses had to be scraped
out of the standing cells
with iron rods

JUDGE: Why
had this man been sentenced

8TH WITNESS: He had tried to escape
Before he was put in the cell
he had to march past
the prisoners
lined up for evening roll call
He had a sign tied to him
that read
HURRAY I'M BACK AGAIN
While he shouted out the words on the sign
he had to beat on a drum
Of those sentenced to the standing cell
Bruno Graf was the prisoner
who lasted the longest
Arrest Supervisor Schlage
used to stand at this door sometimes
when Graf was bellowing in there

and I heard Schlage
yell
Why don't you just die
It took Graf a month to die

JUDGE: Accused Schlage
did you allow prisoners to starve to death
in the standing cells

ACCUSED #14:Mr Chairman
I request permission to say the following
I was
if I may say so
only the lock-up man
I received my orders from my superiors
and I was duty-bound to carry them out
For what took place in the Bunker
I was not responsible
The Chief Arrest Supervisor was responsible

JUDGE: Who brought food to the prisoners

ACCUSED #14:Special-duty prisoners did that

JUDGE: Who locked the cells

ACCUSED #14:Special-duty prisoners did that too
We Arrest Supervisors
were only responsible
for unlocking the outside gates
when the Political Division arrived

JUDGE: Did prisoners
die in the Arrest Bunker

ACCUSED #14: That's possible
But I can't really remember

JUDGE: Who kept the Death Book
and entered causes of death

ACCUSED #14: Only special-duty prisoners did all that

JUDGE: And you had nothing to do

ACCUSED #14: I had our own people to guard
There were sometimes as many
as 18 of them
I had to make
sure
they didn't try to kill themselves
or do some other dumb thing

JUDGE: You mean to say
that members of units serving in the camp
were also jailed in the Bunker

ACCUSED #14: Of course
There was justice for all
Surely Your Honor
every sign of weakness
had to be fought against

THE SONG OF THE BUNKER BLOCK
II

JUDGE: How large were the other cells
in the Bunker

9TH WITNESS: The other cells were roughly
eight feet wide
eight feet long
eight feet high
Some were dark cells
The rest had a small window
with a concrete rim
The only air vent was
high up in the wall
It was an opening no bigger
than the palm of your hand

JUDGE: How many such cells were there

9TH WITNESS: 28 cells

JUDGE: How many prisoners
could be put in a cell

9TH WITNESS: In that space
there were often as many
as 40 prisoners

JUDGE: How long did they have to stay there

9TH WITNESS: Often for several weeks

The prisoner Bogdan Glinski
was in there for more than 17 weeks
from November 13 1942
till March 9 1943

JUDGE: How was the cell furnished

9TH WITNESS: There was only a wooden box
                  with a bucket in it

JUDGE: What regulations applied
                  to prisoners put in these cells

9TH WITNESS: Here too the sentence was either
                  overnight confinement
                  or long-term confinement
                  And here too confinement
                  without food was practiced

JUDGE: Which punishment did you undergo

9TH WITNESS: I spent two nights in there

JUDGE: Would you describe what happened

9TH WITNESS: I had to report at Barrack 11
                  at 9 o'clock at night
                  together with 38 other prisoners
                  The Barrack-elder reported
                  the count
                  to the Barrack-leader on duty
                  Then he took us down to the basement
                  and locked us into Cell 20
                  By 10 o'clock
                  the air was already stifling
                  We stood crowded against each other

We couldn't sit down
and we couldn't lie down
It was soon so hot
we started taking off our jackets
and pants
Around midnight
we couldn't stand any more
Some collapsed
The others hung on to each other
Most of the prisoners were tense
and restless
and shoved and swore
at each other
The smell
from the men who were suffocating
mixed with the stink
coming out of the bucket
The weak got trampled
The stronger fought
to get up next to the door
where a little air came in
We shouted and pounded on the door
We battered and hammered at it
but it didn't give
Once in a while
the peep hole was opened outside
and the jailer on duty
looked in at us
By 2 o'clock in the morning
most of the prisoners
had lost consciousness
At 5
the door was opened
We were pulled out
into the corridor
We were all naked

Of the 38 who went in
19 were still alive
Of these 19
6 were taken to the infirmary
where 4 died

3RD WITNESS: I belonged to the corpse detail
that had to clean out the hunger cells
Frequently
the dead in there had bites
in their buttocks and thighs
Often those
who had held out the longest
had some fingers missing
I asked the Bunker-Jakob
who was in charge of cleaning the Bunker
How can you stand it
He said
Praise be
what makes a man hard
Everything's fine with me
I eat their rations
Their death doesn't move me
All this moves me about as much
as that stone in the wall

THE SONG OF THE BUNKER BLOCK

III

6TH WITNESS: On the 3rd of September 1941
the first experiments
in mass killings
using the gas Cyklon B
were carried out in the Bunker
Staff medical orderlies and guards
brought about 850 Soviet prisoners of war
and 220 prisoner patients
to Barrack 11
After they had been locked in the cells
earth was shoveled against the windows
to seal them off
Then the gas
was funneled in
through the air holes
The next day it was ascertained
that some of the prisoners
were still alive
As a result
another portion of Cyklon B
was poured in
On the 5th of September
I was ordered to report to Barrack 11
together with 20 prisoners
from the penal company
We were told
that we were being sent
on a special work assignment
and that the penalty

for revealing what we saw there
was death
We were also promised extra rations
when the work was done
We were issued gas masks
and had to get
the corpses out of the cells
When we opened the doors
the tight pack of people
fell out against us
Even dead they were still standing
Their faces were blue
Many of them had bunches of hair
in their hands
It took us the whole day
to pry them apart
and stack them in the courtyard
That evening the commanding officer
and his staff
came
I heard the commanding officer say
Now I'm relieved
Now that we have this gas
we'll be spared all those bloodbaths
The victims too
will be spared
until the very last moment

THE SONG OF CYKLON B

I

3RD WITNESS: In the summer and fall of 1941
I worked in the camp's laundry room
That's where dirty laundry was taken
to be fumigated with the gas Cyklon B
Our superior was
the fumigator Breitwieser

JUDGE: Does the witness
see this person
in this room

3RD WITNESS: That is Breitwieser
[Accused #17 nods to the witness agree-
ably]
On September 3rd
I saw Breitwieser
accompanied by Stark
and some other officers
from the Political Division
walking to Barrack 11
with gas masks and cans
Then the curfew sounded
The next morning
Breitwieser was in a bad mood
because something had gone wrong
The place hadn't been sealed off properly
and the gassing
had to be repeated
Two days later

                    trucks loaded with corpses
                    drove off from the courtyard

JUDGE: What time was it when you saw Breitwieser
                    on his way to Barrack 11
                    on September 3rd

3RD WITNESS: About 9 o'clock at night

ACCUSED #17: That's impossible
                    In the first place
                    I was never in the camp at night
                    Secondly nobody
                    could possibly have recognized me
                    at that time of the year
                    since a heavy fog
                    always came up from the river around then

JUDGE: Did you know
                    that prisoners were to be gassed
                    in Barrack 11 that night

ACCUSED #17: Yes
                    that had gotten around

JUDGE: You did not see
                    prisoners being driven into the Barrack

ACCUSED #17: Mr President
                    our workday was over at 6 p m
                    I was never in the camp after 6

JUDGE: You never had to issue clothing
                    after 6 o'clock
                    even if new transports had arrived

228

ACCUSED #17: When prisoners arrived after 6
special-duty prisoners picked up the key
to the changing room
and issued the clothes

JUDGE: What were your duties
as fumigator

ACCUSED #17: If I may say so
I had to give instructions

JUDGE: Had you been trained
for this job

ACCUSED #17: In the summer of 1941
with 10 or 15 others
I was detailed to the fumigation squad
Some men from the Degesch Company
delivered the gas
They also gave us our instructions
They taught us how to use the gas
and how to use the masks
that were equipped
with special headgear

JUDGE: How was the gas packed

ACCUSED #17: It came in cans
a pound each
They looked like coffee cans
At first they had gray cardboard tops
The cardboard was usually slightly moist
Later on they had metal lids

JUDGE: What did the contents look like

ACCUSED #17: It was a grainy crumbly substance
It's hard to describe
It looked something like starch
bluish white

JUDGE: Do you know what this substance
was made of

ACCUSED #17: Hydrocyanic acid
in its chemically bonded form
As soon as the crystals
were exposed to the air
cyanide gas was produced

JUDGE: What did your work with the gas involve

ACCUSED #17: Prisoners had to hang up their clothes
in the changing room
Then I and an assistant threw in the gas
After 24 hours the clothes
were taken out
and new ones brought in
and so on
We also had to fumigate living quarters
After the windows had been sealed
the cans were pried open
and a rubber cover quickly slipped on
Otherwise the gas began to escape
and we still had several more cans
that had to be opened
When everything was ready
the stuff was scattered

JUDGE: Was any warning agent
mixed in with the gas

ACCUSED #17: No
                Cyklon B worked very rapidly
                I remember
                once Corporal Theurer
                went in a house
                that had been fumigated
                During the night
                the ground floor had been aired
                and the next morning Theurer
                went upstairs to the second floor
                to open the windows
                He must have breathed in some fumes
                because he fell over immediately
                rolled down the stairs unconscious
                and right on out
                to where he got some fresh air
                If he had fallen any other way
                he never would have gotten out of there

PROSECUTING
ATTORNEY: With your professional experience
                were you not called in as an adviser
                when Cyklon B began to be used
                on prisoners

ACCUSED #17: I speak nothing but the truth
                as a matter of principle
                I could not stand the gas
                It gave me indigestion
                I applied for transfer

PROSECUTING
ATTORNEY: Were you transferred

ACCUSED #17: Not right away
PROSECUTING
ATTORNEY: When were you transferred

ACCUSED #17: I don't remember that any more

PROSECUTING
ATTORNEY: You were transferred in April 1944
Before then you were promoted twice
Your first promotion
was to private first class
then to corporal

COUNSEL FOR
THE DEFENSE: We object
to the prosecution's insinuations
The fact that members of the camp staff
were promoted
must be judged only within the context
of their military duty
In no way does it prove complicity
[*The Accused show their agreement*]

THE SONG OF CYKLON B

II

JUDGE: Where was the gas stored

6TH WITNESS: It was stored in crates
                          in the dispensary basement

JUDGE: Accused Capesius
                          as head of the dispensary
                          were you aware that Cyklon B
                          was stored there

ACCUSED #3:   I believe
                          the witness is the victim
                          of some confusion here
                          In regard to those crates in the basement
                          they contained Ovaltine
                          They were a shipment from the Swiss
                          Red Cross

6TH WITNESS: I saw the cases of Ovaltine
                          and I saw the crates of Cyklon
                          and I also saw the suitcases
                          where the accused Capesius
                          kept jewelry and gold fillings

ACCUSED #3:   This is a complete fabrication

6TH WITNESS: Where did the money come from
                          which made it possible
                          for the accused Capesius

to open his own pharmacy
and a beauty parlor
immediately after the war
Be beautiful
with beauty treatments by Capesius
That was his firm's advertisement

ACCUSED #3: I obtained this money by taking out a loan

6TH WITNESS: And where do the 12,500 dollars come from
that were offered to me
and other witnesses
if we would testify here
that Capesius
was only in charge of the dispensary
and was not in charge of
the phenol and Cyklon B

ACCUSED #3: I don't know anything about that
PROSECUTING
ATTORNEY: Who made this attempt to bribe you

6TH WITNESS: It came from an anonymous source
PROSECUTING
ATTORNEY: Do you know
whether any of the legal-aid societies
of the camp guards
were behind the bribe

6TH WITNESS: I don't know
However I would like to call
to the attention of the court
this letter
which was sent to me
The heading of the letter reads
Working Committee for Justice and Freedom

The letter itself
You will soon disappear
You will die an agonizing death
Our people are keeping you
under constant observation
You can choose now
Life or death

JUDGE: The court will take this matter
under investigation

COUNSEL FOR
THE DEFENSE: Can the witness
tell us what was printed on the crates

6TH WITNESS: Caution
Poison gas
There was also a warning label
with a skull and crossbones

COUNSEL FOR
THE DEFENSE: Did you see what was in the crates

6TH WITNESS: I saw opened crates
with the cans inside

COUNSEL FOR
THE DEFENSE: What was on the labels

6TH WITNESS: Poison gas
Cyklon

COUNSEL FOR
THE DEFENSE: Was there anything else on the labels

6TH WITNESS: Caution
Contains no warning agent
To be opened only by experienced personnel

JUDGE: Did the witness

see these cans actually
being taken to the gas chambers

6TH WITNESS: We had to load the crates
into the ambulance
that came around to pick it up

JUDGE: Who rode in that ambulance

6TH WITNESS: I saw Dr Frank and Dr Schatz
as well as Dr Capesius
They had their gas masks with them
Dr Schatz was wearing his steel helmet
I remember that
because somebody in the car
laughed and said
You look like a little toadstool

COUNSEL FOR
THE DEFENSE: We would like to remind the court
that at certain times during the war
the wearing of gas masks was mandatory
Neither the coming or going of our clients
with gas masks
proves anything about where they had gone

JUDGE: Did the witness
see delivery receipts
for gas shipments

6TH WITNESS: When these shipments arrived
I was often assigned
to take the accompanying bills
to the administration
The shipments grew increasingly large
and finally had to be stored
outside the camp in the old theater

236

The sender was
The Blight Prevention Company

JUDGE: How were these shipments
forwarded to the camp

6TH WITNESS: Some were trucked in
directly from the factory
Others came in by rail
on army bills of lading

JUDGE: Do you recall the amounts declared

6TH WITNESS: 14 to 20 crates
came in at a time

JUDGE: According to your calculations
how often did these shipments arrive

6TH WITNESS: At least once a week
In 1944
several times a week
Then trucks from the motor pool
were called in to help out

JUDGE: How many cans
were in a crate

6TH WITNESS: Each crate held 30 one-pound cans

JUDGE: Was the price marked

6TH WITNESS: The price was 50 cents a pound

JUDGE: How many pounds
were required for a single gassing

6TH WITNESS: For 2000 people in one chamber
about 16 pounds

JUDGE: At 50 cents per pound
8 dollars

THE SONG OF CYKLON B

III

JUDGE: Accused Mulka
as camp adjutant
you were in charge of the motor pool
Did you write up
the transportation orders

ACCUSED #1: I wrote no such orders
I had nothing to do with that

JUDGE: Did you know the meaning of the phrase
Requisitions for Material for Relocation

ACCUSED #1: No

JUDGE: Accused Mulka
the court has in its possession orders
for the transportation of Material for Reloca-
    tion
These documents bear your signature

ACCUSED #1: It is possible
that I may have had to sign
some such order occasionally

JUDGE: You never found out
that Material for Relocation
was in fact the gas Cyklon B

ACCUSED #1: As I already said
I wasn't aware of that

JUDGE: Who issued requisitions for this material

ACCUSED #1: They came in over the teletype
and were then passed on
to the commanding officer
or a protective-custody camp leader
They were sent on from there
to the head of the motor pool

JUDGE: Weren't you in charge there

ACCUSED #1: Only in disciplinary matters

JUDGE: But weren't you concerned
to know
to what use trucks from your motor pool
were being put

ACCUSED #1: I knew of course
that they were required
for the transport of material

JUDGE: Were prisoners also
transported in these trucks

ACCUSED #1: I don't know anything about that
In my time
prisoners walked

JUDGE: Accused Mulka
the court has in its possession a document
which deals with
the urgently required completion
of the new crematoriums
It also refers to the fact that
the prisoners used for this project

were required to work on Sundays as well
The document bears your signature

ACCUSED #1:   Yes
              well
              I must have dictated it then

JUDGE: Do you still maintain
              you knew nothing
              about the mass killings

ACCUSED #1:   All my previous statements
              conform to the truth

JUDGE: The court has summoned as witness
              the former chief mechanic
              of the motor-pool repair shop
              Will the witness tell us
              how many trucks there were
              in the motor pool

1ST WITNESS: For heavy duty
              there were ten 2½-ton trucks

JUDGE: From whom did you receive
              your transportation orders

1ST WITNESS: From the head of the motor pool

JUDGE: Who signed the orders

1ST WITNESS: I don't know

JUDGE: What were the trucks used for

1ST WITNESS: For picking up freight
              and transporting prisoners

JUDGE: Where were the prisoners taken

1ST WITNESS: I can't say for sure

JUDGE: Did you take part
                  in any of these transports

1ST WITNESS: I had to go along once
                  as a replacement

JUDGE: Where did you go

1ST WITNESS: Into the camp
                  where they picked them out
                  and so on

JUDGE: Where did you take them

1ST WITNESS: To the far end of the camp
                  There were woods over there
                  a birch wood
                  That's where the people were unloaded

JUDGE: Where did they go

1ST WITNESS: Into a house
                  I didn't see anything else after that

JUDGE: What happened to the people

1ST WITNESS: I don't know
                  I wasn't in there

JUDGE: Didn't you find out
                  what happened to them

1ST WITNESS: Well
yes
They were burned up
right then and there

THE SONG OF THE FIRE OVENS

I

JUDGE: The witness
drove one of the ambulances
that carried
Cyklon B in its solid state
to the gas chambers

2ND WITNESS: I was originally assigned to the camp
as a tractor driver
Later on I had to drive an ambulance too

JUDGE: Where did you have to drive

2ND WITNESS: I had to pick up
the medical orderlies and the doctors

JUDGE: Who were the doctors

2ND WITNESS: I can't remember

JUDGE: Where did you have to take them

2ND WITNESS: From the old camp
to the arrival platform in the new camp

JUDGE: When

2ND WITNESS: When transports arrived

JUDGE: How were transport arrivals announced

2ND WITNESS: By a siren

JUDGE: Where did you drive to
from the arrival platform

2ND WITNESS: To the crematoriums

JUDGE: Did the doctors go with you

2ND WITNESS: Yes

JUDGE: What did they do there

2ND WITNESS: The doctors stayed in the ambulance
or stood around outside
The medical orderlies had to
take care of everything

JUDGE: What did they have to take care of

2ND WITNESS: The gassings

JUDGE: When you got there
were the people already
in the gas chambers

2ND WITNESS: They were still getting undressed

JUDGE: Was there ever any trouble

2ND WITNESS: The times I was there
things always went smoothly

JUDGE: What could you see
of the gassing procedure

2ND WITNESS: When the prisoners had been taken
into the chambers
the orderlies went up to the vents
put on their gas masks
and emptied their cans

JUDGE: Where were these vents

2ND WITNESS: There was an embankment that went up
and over the underground room
It had four compartments

JUDGE: How many cans were emptied

2ND WITNESS: Three or four
in each hole

JUDGE: How long did this take

2ND WITNESS: About a minute

JUDGE: Didn't the people scream

2ND WITNESS: When one of them realized
what was going on
yes
you could hear a scream

PROSECUTING
ATTORNEY: How far from the gas chamber
was your ambulance parked

2ND WITNESS: It was on the road
about 20 yards off

PROSECUTING
ATTORNEY: And from there you could hear
what was happening down in the chambers

2ND WITNESS: Sometimes I got out
to wait around outside

PROSECUTING
ATTORNEY: What did you do there

2ND WITNESS: Nothing
I smoked a cigarette

PROSECUTING
ATTORNEY: Did you ever get near the vents
above the gas chamber

2ND WITNESS: Sometimes I walked up and down a bit
to stretch my legs

PROSECUTING
ATTORNEY: What did you hear

2ND WITNESS: When they took the lids off the vents
I heard a humming from down there
as if a lot of people were underground

PROSECUTING
ATTORNEY: And what did you do then

2ND WITNESS: The vents were shut again
and I had to drive back

JUDGE: You were prisoner doctor
in the Special Commando
assigned to duty at the crematoriums
How many prisoners
were in that Commando

7TH WITNESS: A total of 860 men
Each Special Commando was destroyed
after a few months
and replaced by a new crew

247

JUDGE: Under whom did you serve

7TH WITNESS: Dr Mengele

JUDGE: How did the delivery of prisoners
              to the gas chambers proceed

7TH WITNESS: A whistle from the locomotive
              on its way from the platform to the gate
              was the signal
              that a new shipment had arrived
              That meant
              that inside an hour
              the ovens had to be fully operational
              The electric motors were switched on
              These started up the fans
              that brought the fire in the ovens
              up to the required temperature

JUDGE: Could you see
              the groups coming off the arrival platform

7TH WITNESS: From the window in my workroom
              I could see the upper half of the platform
              and the road to the crematorium
              The people arrived five abreast
              The sick came behind in the trucks
              The crematorium area
              was closed off by an iron fence
              There were warnings posted at the gate
              The accompanying guards had to stop there
              and the Special Commando took over
              Only doctors staff orderlies
              and members of the Political Division
              were allowed in

248

JUDGE: Which of the accused
did you see there

7TH WITNESS: I saw Stark there and Hofmann
also Kaduk and Baretzki

COUNSEL FOR
THE DEFENSE: We call attention to the fact
that our clients
deny having participated in these events

JUDGE: Will the witness continue his account

7TH WITNESS: The people
went through the gate slowly and wearily
Children hung on to their mother's skirts
Old men carried babies
or pushed baby carriages
The path was covered with black cinders
and on the grass on each side of the path
there were pipes with water faucets
The people crowded around them
and the Commando let them drink
but hurried them on
There was still about 60 yards to go
before they got to the stairs
that led down to the anteroom

JUDGE: Was there an unobstructed view
of the crematorium

7TH WITNESS: It was surrounded by bushes and trees
and was set back about 100 yards away
from the fence surrounding the area
Beyond that fence was the outer fence
with observation towers
Back of them were open fields

JUDGE: What could be seen
of the crematorium installations

7TH WITNESS: Only the incineration building
with its large square chimney
Underground it was connected
by a corridor
that led to the gas chambers
and branched off
to the anteroom

JUDGE: How large was the anteroom

7TH WITNESS: About 50 yards long
Some 12 to 15 steps led down to it
The room was over six feet high
In the middle
there was a row of supporting columns

JUDGE: How many people were taken down at a time

7TH WITNESS: From one to two thousand people

JUDGE: Did they know
what lay before them

7TH WITNESS: At the head of the narrow staircase
there were signs
that said in various languages
BATH AND DISINFECTION ROOM
That sounded reassuring
and calmed a lot of people
who were still mistrustful
I often saw people
go down there quite happily
and mothers joked with their children

JUDGE: Was there never any outbreak of panic
                with so many people
                in such a small place

7TH WITNESS: Everything always went quickly
                and smoothly
                The command to undress was given
                and while the people were still
                looking around bewildered
                the Special Commando began to
                help them off
                with their clothes
                There were benches along the walls
                with numbered pegs over them
                It was repeatedly announced
                that clothes and shoes
                must be hung on the peg
                and that its number
                must not be forgotten
                to avoid unnecessary confusion
                upon return from the bath
                In the glaring light of that room
                the people took off their clothes
                Men and women
                old and young
                Children

JUDGE: Did this great number of people
                never once
                attack their guards

7TH WITNESS: Only once did I hear
                somebody shout
                They're going to kill us
                But somebody answered
                That's impossible

That can't happen
Keep calm
And when children started crying
their parents comforted them
and joked and played with them
as they carried them
into the next room

JUDGE: Where was the entrance to that room

7TH WITNESS: At the end of the anteroom
It was a solid oak door
with a peep hole
and a hand-wheel
that screwed the door shut

JUDGE: How long did the undressing take

7TH WITNESS: About 10 minutes
Then they were all shoved
into the next room

JUDGE: Was force ever used

7TH WITNESS: The men in the Special Commando shouted
Move step it up
the water's getting cold
Naturally there were also
threats and beatings
or one of the guards
would fire a shot

JUDGE: Was this other room
equipped with showers
or disguised in any way

7TH WITNESS: No
There was nothing

JUDGE: How big was this room

7TH WITNESS: Smaller than the anteroom
About 30 yards long

JUDGE: Certainly with 1000 or more people crowded
into such a small space
there must have been some disturbance

7TH WITNESS: It was too late then
The last ones were pushed in
and the door screwed shut

JUDGE: Can the witness
offer any explanation
why the people permitted
all this to happen to them
Faced with that room
they must have known
they were facing death

7TH WITNESS: No one had ever come out
to tell about it

JUDGE: Once they were in
what did they see

7TH WITNESS: There were concrete walls
and some valves on the walls
In the middle of the room were the pillars
and on each side two posts
made out of perforated sheet iron

There were drains in the floor
This room too was brightly lit

JUDGE: What could be heard
                  from the people in there

7TH WITNESS: They began to scream
                  and they pounded on the door
                  but you couldn't hear much
                  because of the strong roar
                  that came from the cremation room

JUDGE: What could be seen
                  through the window in the door

7TH WITNESS: The people crowded the door
                  and climbed up the pillars
                  They began to suffocate
                  when the gas was thrown in

THE SONG OF THE FIRE OVENS

II

7TH WITNESS: The gas was poured
into the sheet-iron posts from up above
There was a spiral channel
inside the post
which spread the substance
In the moist hot air
it rapidly turned to gas
and poured out through the holes

JUDGE: How long did it take the gas
to kill

7TH WITNESS: That depended on the amount used
For reasons of economy usually
a less than adequate amount was poured in
so that the killing
could take as long as five minutes

JUDGE: What was the immediate effect of the gas

7TH WITNESS: It induced dizziness and severe nausea
and made breathing extremely difficult

JUDGE: How long was the room kept under gas

7TH WITNESS: 20 minutes
Then the ventilation system was turned on
and the gas pumped out
30 minutes later the doors were opened

But there was still gas
caught in small pockets
among the dead
which caused a dry hacking cough
For this reason
the men in the Clearance Detail
had to wear gas masks

JUDGE: Did you
see this room after the door
had been opened

7TH WITNESS: Yes
The corpses lay piled on top of each other
near the door and around the columns
Babies children and the sick at the bottom
Women above them
And at the very top the strongest men
The reason for this
was that the people trampled
and climbed on each other
because the gas initially spread
most thickly at floor level
The people clawing each other
were stuck together
Their skin was torn
Many were bleeding from nose and mouth
The faces were swollen
and spotted
The heaps of people were befouled
with vomit
excrement urine and menstrual blood
The Clearance Detail came in with hoses
and washed the corpses down
Then they were pulled
into the freight elevators
and taken up to the ovens

JUDGE: How large were these elevators

7TH WITNESS: There were two of them
                each with a capacity of 25 dead
                When one load was in
                a bell was rung
                to signal the Lugging Detail
                that was standing by with carts
                on the floor above
                They had thongs
                that they slipped over the wrists of the dead
                The corpses were then lugged in the carts
                to the ovens on a special track
                Blood was washed away
                by a steady stream of water
                Before cremation
                men of the Special Commando
                conducted a final search
                Every ornament still
                to be found on the bodies
                was removed
                bracelets
                neck chains
                rings
                earrings
                Then the hair was cut off
                and immediately bundled
                and packed
                Finally
                the teeth extractors set to work
                They were a crew picked
                from first-class specialists
                at Dr Mengele's express command
                Still when they started in
                with their crowbars and tongs
                they tore out not only gold teeth
                and bridges

but whole chunks of jaw
These pieces of bone and attached flesh
were thrown into an acid vat
to be eaten away
100 men worked continually
in two shifts
at the ovens

JUDGE: How many ovens were there
in the crematorium

7TH WITNESS: There were five ovens each
in the big crematoriums II and III
Each oven had three incinerating chambers
Beside these two crematoriums
at the end of the Arrival Platform
there were crematoriums IV and V
each with two four-chambered ovens
These two were set off about
800 yards back of the birch grove
When the operation was going full blast
46 incinerating chambers
were fired up

JUDGE: How many bodies
could be put into one chamber

7TH WITNESS: From three to five bodies
could be put in one chamber
However it was rare
that all ovens operated at one time
since they were often damaged
by overheating

JUDGE: How long did cremation take
in an oven chamber

7TH WITNESS: Approximately an hour
Then it could take a new load
In crematoriums II and III
more than 3000 people were cremated
in less than 24 hours
If the ovens were overcrowded
corpses were also burned in a ditch
that had been dug outside the building
These ditches were
about 100 feet long
and 20 feet deep
At each end there were drainage trenches
for the fat
The fat was ladled up in cans
and poured over the corpses
to make them burn faster
In the summer of 1944
when the cremations reached their peak
up to 20,000 people
were destroyed
daily
Their ashes were trucked off
to a river a mile and a half away
and dumped into the water

JUDGE: What was done with the valuables
and gold fillings

1ST WITNESS: When the clothes were collected
money and ornaments found among them
were dropped into a slot in the top
of a locked crate
Guards filled their own pockets first
Clothes and shoes
that the prisoners themselves
had carefully bundled together

were sent home
for the benefit of people
bombed out of their houses
Gold fillings were melted down
I was called in as examining magistrate
because packages sent from the camp
containing gold by the pound
had been confiscated
In the course of my investigation
I ascertained that this was dental gold
Calculating from the weight
of a single filling
I came to the conclusion
that thousands of people were required
to supply even one such nugget

JUDGE: Do you mean
                that even in those times
                a magistrate was called in from outside
                to conduct an investigation in the camp

1ST WITNESS: Somewhere some idea of justice
                still survived
                The commanding officer
                wanted to combat corruption in the camp
                At the time of my visit there
                he complained
                that the men under his command
                frequently failed to rise to the demands
                made on them by their hard work
                Then he took me to a crematorium installation
                where he explained
                everything to me in great detail
                Inside in the cremation rooms everything
                was polished to a shine
                There was nothing to indicate

that people were cremated there
There wasn't even a speck of their dust
on the oven panels
The guards in their room sat
on a bench half drunk
and in the service room
women prisoners
especially picked for their beauty
were baking potato dumplings
which they served the men
When I made a search of their lockers
they proved
to contain a fortune
As judge I instituted proceedings
for theft
and some of them were arrested
and sentenced

JUDGE: How were these proceedings carried out

1ST WITNESS: It was a mock trial
              You could go up only so high
              and it was impossible
              to institute proceedings
              for multiple murder

JUDGE: As examining magistrate
              you saw no means
              of making your findings public

1ST WITNESS: Before what court
              could I have brought an action
              for the killings of masses of people
              and the seizure of their goods and property
              by the highest administrative offices

I could not institute proceedings
against the government itself

JUDGE: Was there no other way
of acting on this matter

1ST WITNESS: I knew
no one would have believed
what I had to say
I would have been executed
or at the very least
locked up in an asylum
I considered fleeing the country
but I doubted whether
even abroad
anyone would believe me
and I asked myself what would happen
if I were believed
and I were called upon to testify
against my own people
and I could only conclude
that this my people would be destroyed
for its deeds
So I stayed

THE SONG OF THE FIRE OVENS

III

JUDGE: There has been testimony of an uprising
carried out by the Special Commando
When did this uprising occur

7TH WITNESS: On October 6 1944
The Commando was to be liquidated
by the guards that day

JUDGE: Did the Commando know this beforehand

7TH WITNESS: They all knew
they were going to be killed
Weeks before
they had obtained cans of explosives
from prisoners who worked
in the armaments factory
The plan was
to first take care of the guards
then blow up the crematoriums
and escape
But the crematorium
where the explosives were stored
blew up earlier than planned
and many of the men
went up with it
There was a battle
but they were all overpowered
Hundreds of prisoners lay
face down on the ground

behind the birch grove
The men from the Political Division
shot them in the back of the head

JUDGE: Which of the accused were present

7TH WITNESS: Boger was in charge

JUDGE: Was this crematorium
destroyed by the explosion

7TH WITNESS: The explosion from four barrels of dynamite
blew up one entire building

JUDGE: What happened to the other crematoriums

7TH WITNESS: They were blown up
by staff personnel shortly after
The front was getting close

PROSECUTING
ATTORNEY: Does the witness
find it credible
that the adjutant
of the camp's commanding officer
was not informed
about what went on in the crematoriums

7TH WITNESS: No
It was impossible
Each one of the 6000 camp staff personnel
knew what was taking place
and each at his post did
what was required
for the functioning of the whole
Furthermore every locomotive engineer
every switchman

every railroad employee
who had anything to do
with the transportation of the people
knew what went on in the camp
Every telegraph clerk and typist
who passed on the Deportation Orders
knew
Every single one
of the hundreds and
thousands of office workers
connected with the widespread operation
knew
what it was all about

COUNSEL FOR
THE DEFENSE: We object to these statements
which are dictated by sheer hate
Hate must never
form the basis
for a judgment
of the particulars under consideration here

7TH WITNESS: I do not speak from hate
I have no desire for revenge
I am not concerned here
with the individual accused
but only wish to bring to mind
that what they did
could not have been carried out
without the support
of millions of others

COUNSEL FOR
THE DEFENSE: This proceeding is strictly confined
to what can be substantiated by proof
against our clients
General charges
are irrelevant

Especially charges
directed against an entire nation
which at that time was engaged
in a great and sacrificial war

7TH WITNESS: I only
want to point out if I may
how many spectators lined the way
when we were driven from our homes
and loaded into freight cars
The accused in these proceedings
were only the last
in a long line

PROSECUTING
ATTORNEY: Can the witness
tell us how many people
in his estimation
were killed
in total
in the camp

7TH WITNESS: Of the 9 million 600 thousand persecuted
who lived in the regions
ruled by their persecutors
6 million have disappeared
and it can be taken for granted
that most of them
were deliberately destroyed
Those who were not shot
beaten to death
tortured to death
or gassed
died of hunger disease and misery
or of being worked to death
Yet to arrive at the sum total
of the defenseless sacrificed

in this war of extermination
we must add to the 6 million
killed for racial reasons
3 million Russian prisoners of war
shot or starved to death
as well as the 10 million civilians
of the occupied countries
who perished

COUNSEL FOR
THE DEFENSE: Even though we all feel
most deeply for the victims
still it is our duty here
to counter and oppose
all exaggerations
and vilification
originating from certain parties
In relation to this camp
not even the sum of 2 million dead
can be conclusively established
Only the death of several hundred thousand
can be proven
The majority of the groups named
ended up in the east
and those seized
and liquidated
as armed units
cannot be counted among the murdered
nor can those who deserted
to enemy armies and fell in battle
During the course of these proceedings
it has become all too clear
which political point of view
has determined
the accusations of the witnesses
accusations which the witnesses certainly
had sufficient time

to work out among themselves
> [*The Accused laugh nodding in
> agreement*]

PROSECUTING
ATTORNEY: This is a willful and conscious expression
of contempt
for those who died in the camp
and for those survivors
who have appeared here
to testify as witnesses
The behavior of the counsel for the defense
clearly demonstrates the persistence
of that same outlook
of which the accused present were guilty

COUNSEL FOR
THE DEFENSE: Who is this assistant prosecutor
with his unsuitable clothes
It is I believe a Middle European custom
to appear in court with a closed robe

JUDGE: The court calls for order
Accused Mulka
will you now tell us
what you knew
about the Extermination Program
and what orders you issued
in this connection

ACCUSED #1: I issued no orders connected with that

JUDGE: You knew nothing
about the Extermination Program

ACCUSED #1: Only toward the end of my time in the service
I can say now
that I was filled with revulsion

JUDGE: If this was the case
                  Why did you not refuse
                  to participate

ACCUSED #1:   I was an officer
                  and knew the military penal code

PROSECUTING
ATTORNEY: You were not an officer

ACCUSED #1:   I certainly was
PROSECUTING
ATTORNEY: You were not an officer
                  You belonged to a uniformed
                  Murder Commando

ACCUSED #1:   You are attacking my honor
PROSECUTING
ATTORNEY: Accused Mulka
                  we are dealing with murder

ACCUSED #1:   We were convinced
                  that our orders
                  were all part of achieving some secret
                  military objective
                  Mr President I almost broke down
                  The whole business made me so sick I
                  had to be hospitalized
                  But I want to make it clear
                  that I only looked on from the outside
                  and that I
                  kept my own hands out of it
                  Your Honor I was against
                  the whole thing
                  I myself was
                  persecuted by the system

JUDGE: What happened to you

ACCUSED #1: I was arrested
             because I had expressed
             defeatist opinions
             I was in prison for three months
             After my release
             I was caught in an enemy attack
             As an old soldier
             I was able to save many lives
             by helping with the evacuations
             My own son was killed
             Mr President at this trial
             the millions who also lost their lives
             for their own country
             should not be forgotten
             and what happened after the war
             shouldn't be forgotten either
             and all the things
             that are still being done against us
             All of us
             I want to make that very clear
             did nothing but our duty
             even when that duty was hard
             and even when it grieved us to do it
             Today
             when our nation has worked its way up
             after a devastating war
             to a leading position in the world
             we ought to concern ourselves
             with other things
             than blame and reproaches
             that should be thought of
             as long since atoned for
                  [*Loud approbation from the Accused*]

END

PETER WEISS

Peter Weiss, playwright, novelist, painter and film director, was born at Nowawes, near Berlin, but left Germany when Nazism came in. He has lived in Sweden ever since, although he continues to write in German.

His experimental films have been shown in this country, and his two autobiographical novels will be issued soon in a single-volume edition.

His previous play, *The Persecution and Assassination of Jean-Paul Marat as Performed by the Inmates of the Asylum of Charenton Under the Direction of the Marquis de Sade,* was an international success and in this country won the major awards of the 1965-66 season on Broadway. *The Investigation* was given simultaneous productions in sixteen German cities late in 1965.